SUPERMAN GEN THIRTEEN ™

story
am Hughes

pencils
Lee Bermejo

inks
John Nyberg

letters
Mike Heisler

colors
Guy Major, Ben Dimagmaliw,
& Ian Hannin

riginal series editor
Eric DeSantis

collected edition editor
Neal J. Pozner

book design
Amber Bennett

Superman created by Jerry Siegel & Joe Shuster
Gen[13] created by Jim Lee, J. Scott Campbell & Brandon Choi
Cover by Lee Bermejo

ERMAN/GEN13. Published by WildStorm Productions, an imprint of DC Comics. Editorial offices 7910 Ivanhoe Ave. #438 La Jolla, CA 92037.
r and compilation copyright © 2001 DC Comics. All Rights Reserved. Originally published in single magazine form as SUPERMAN/GEN13 1-3.
yright © 2000 DC COMICS. All rights reserved. All characters, their distinctive likenesses and related indicia featured in this publication are
emarks of DC Comics. The stories, characters, and incidents featured in this publication are entirely fictional. Printed in Canada
N: 1-56389-767-9 DC Comics. A division of Warner Bros. - An AOL Time Warner Company

Cover Gallery

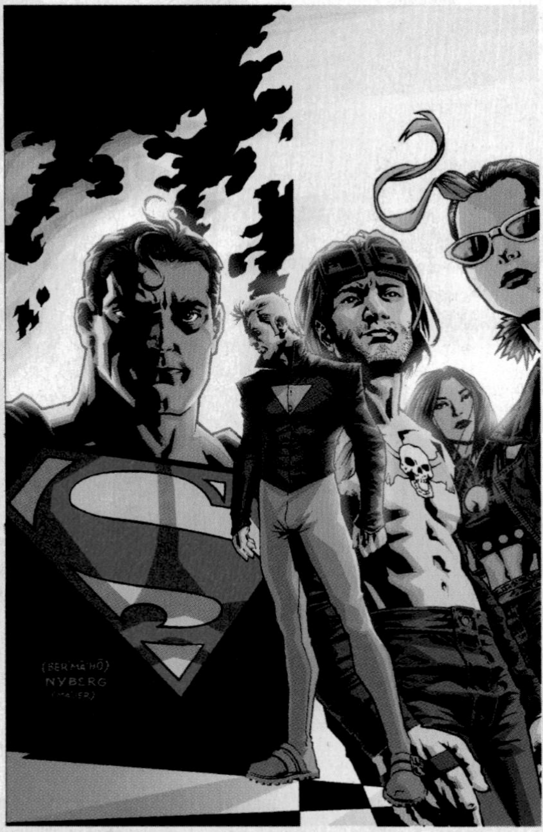

Superman/Gen[13] #2 cover by Lee Bermejo, John Nyberg & Guy Major

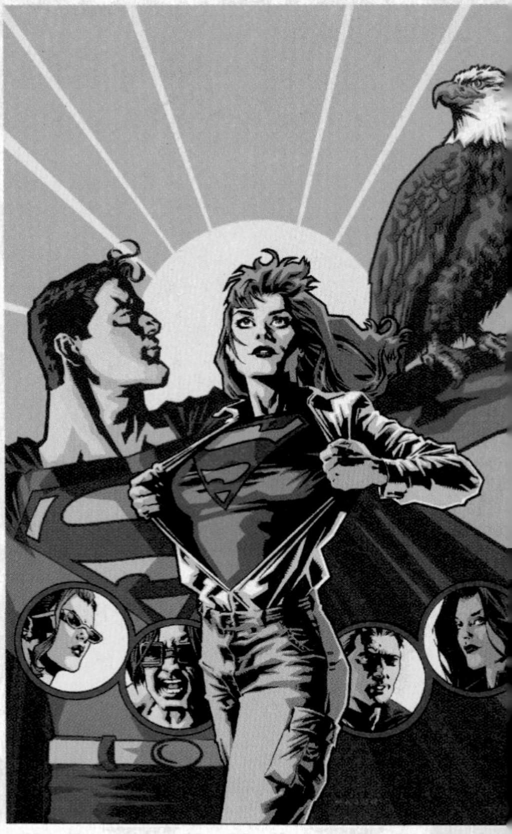

Superman/Gen[13] #1 cover by Lee Bermejo, John Nyberg Guy Major

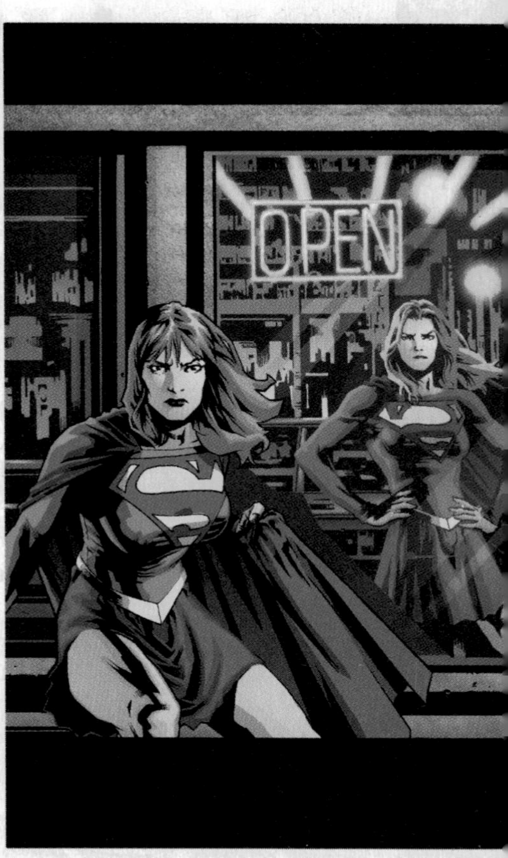
OPEN

Superman/Gen[13] #3 cover by Lee Bermejo, John Nyberg Wendy Fouts

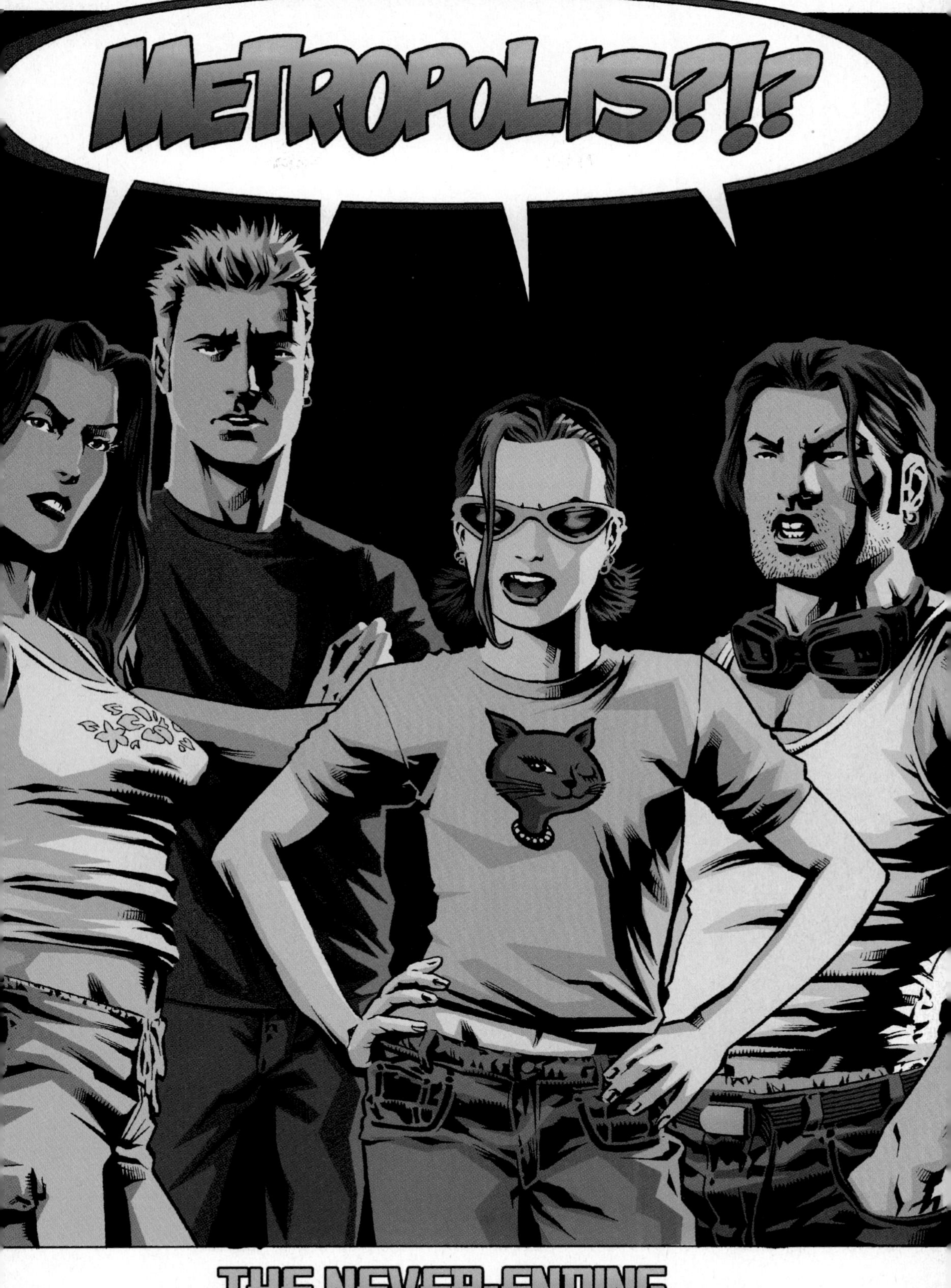
METROPOLIS?!?

THE NEVER-ENDING PRATTLE

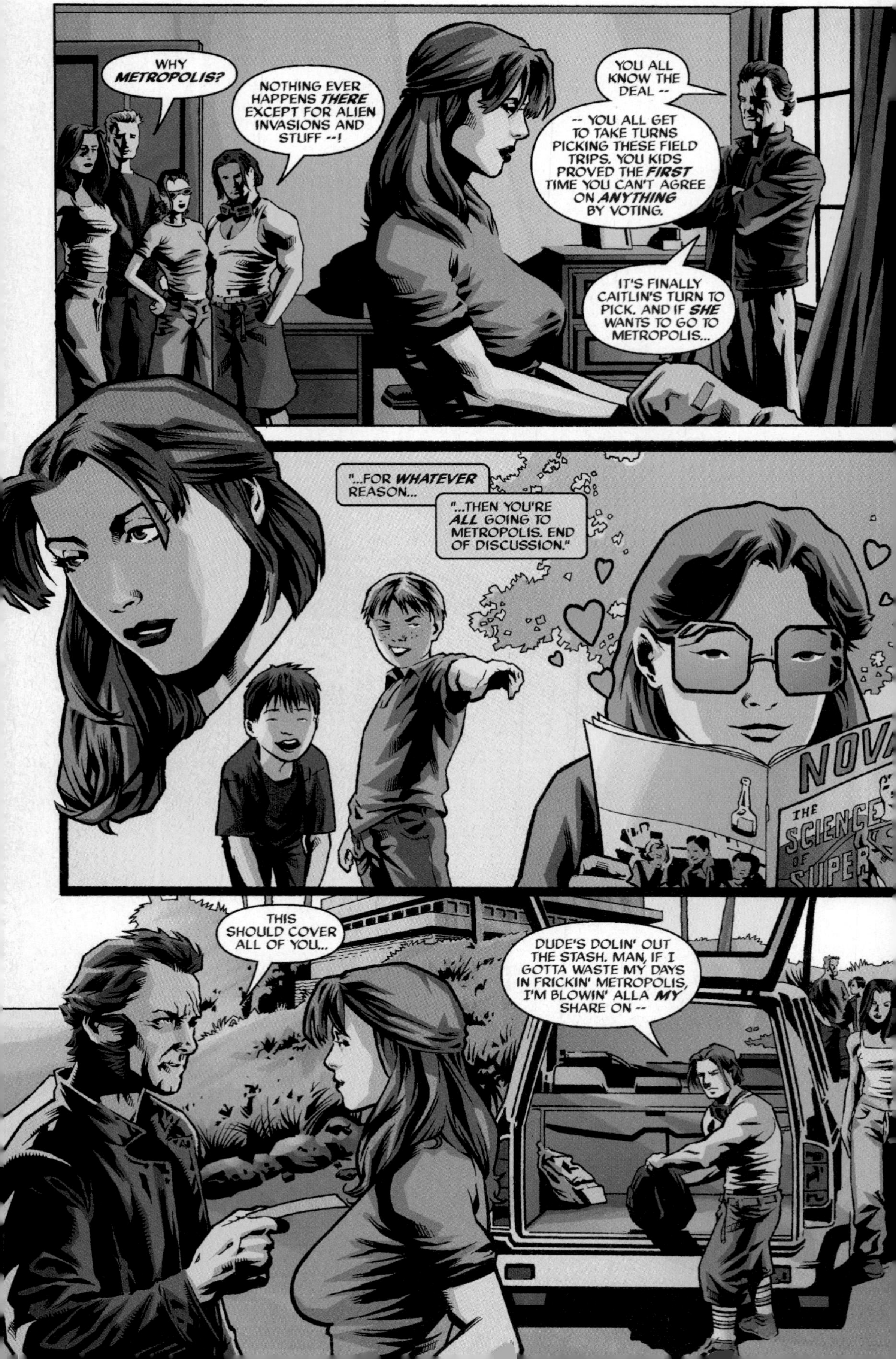
WHY METROPOLIS?
NOTHING EVER HAPPENS THERE EXCEPT FOR ALIEN INVASIONS AND STUFF --!
YOU ALL KNOW THE DEAL --
-- YOU ALL GET TO TAKE TURNS PICKING THESE FIELD TRIPS. YOU KIDS PROVED THE FIRST TIME YOU CAN'T AGREE ON ANYTHING BY VOTING.
IT'S FINALLY CAITLIN'S TURN TO PICK. AND IF SHE WANTS TO GO TO METROPOLIS...
"...FOR WHATEVER REASON...
"...THEN YOU'RE ALL GOING TO METROPOLIS. END OF DISCUSSION."
NOVA
THE SCIENCE OF SUPER
THIS SHOULD COVER ALL OF YOU...
DUDE'S DOLIN' OUT THE STASH. MAN, IF I GOTTA WASTE MY DAYS IN FRICKIN' METROPOLIS, I'M BLOWIN' ALLA MY SHARE ON --

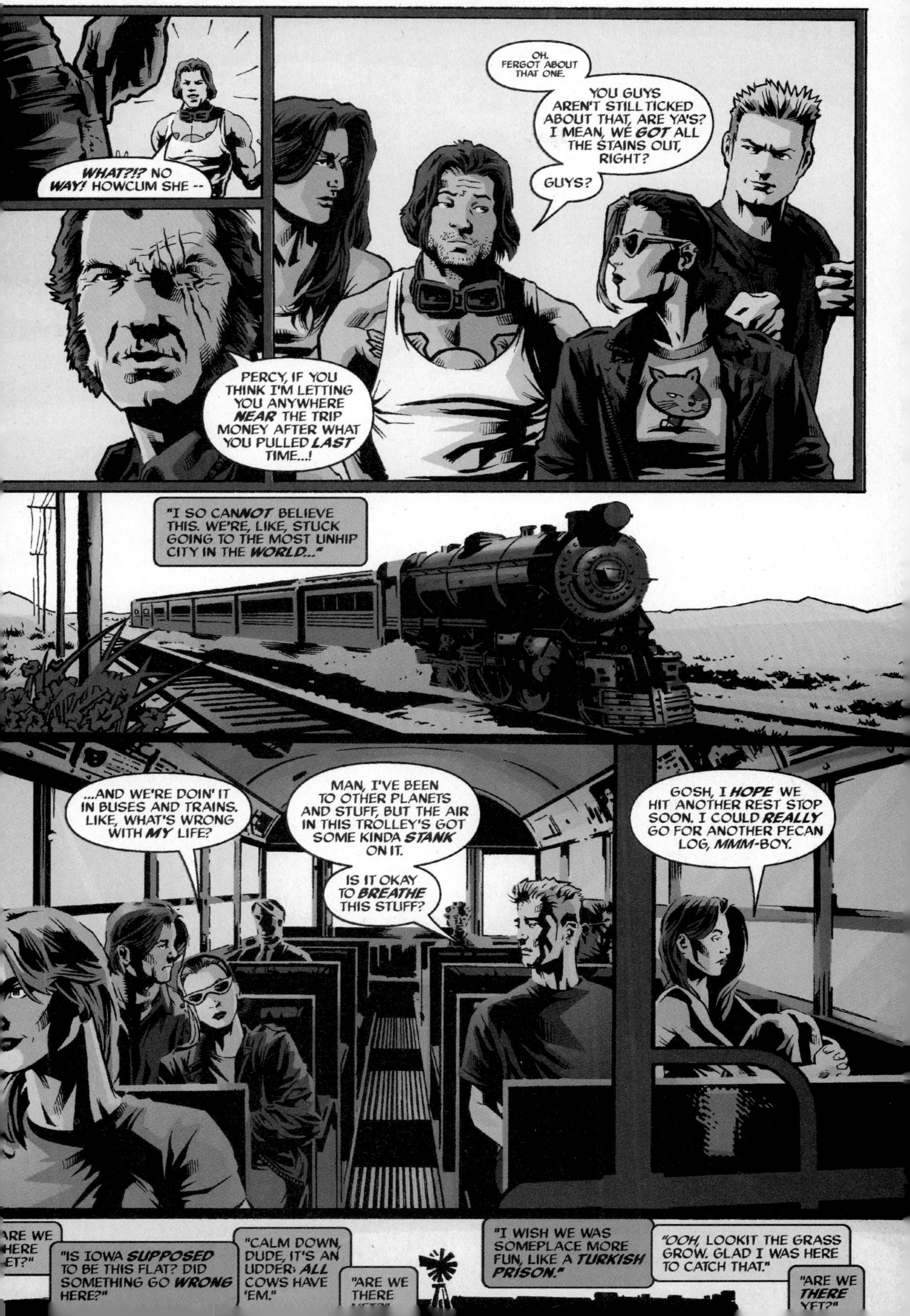
WHAT?!? NO WAY! HOWCUM SHE --
PERCY, IF YOU THINK I'M LETTING YOU ANYWHERE NEAR THE TRIP MONEY AFTER WHAT YOU PULLED LAST TIME...!
OH. FERGOT ABOUT THAT ONE.
YOU GUYS AREN'T STILL TICKED ABOUT THAT, ARE YA'S? I MEAN, WE GOT ALL THE STAINS OUT, RIGHT?
GUYS?
"I SO CANNOT BELIEVE THIS. WE'RE, LIKE, STUCK GOING TO THE MOST UNHIP CITY IN THE WORLD..."
...AND WE'RE DOIN' IT IN BUSES AND TRAINS. LIKE, WHAT'S WRONG WITH MY LIFE?
MAN, I'VE BEEN TO OTHER PLANETS AND STUFF, BUT THE AIR IN THIS TROLLEY'S GOT SOME KINDA STANK ON IT.
IS IT OKAY TO BREATHE THIS STUFF?
GOSH, I HOPE WE HIT ANOTHER REST STOP SOON. I COULD REALLY GO FOR ANOTHER PECAN LOG, MMM-BOY.
"IS IOWA SUPPOSED TO BE THIS FLAT? DID SOMETHING GO WRONG HERE?"
"CALM DOWN, DUDE, IT'S AN UDDER: ALL COWS HAVE 'EM."
"I WISH WE WAS SOMEPLACE MORE FUN, LIKE A TURKISH PRISON."
"OOH, LOOKIT THE GRASS GROW. GLAD I WAS HERE TO CATCH THAT."
"ARE WE THERE YET?"

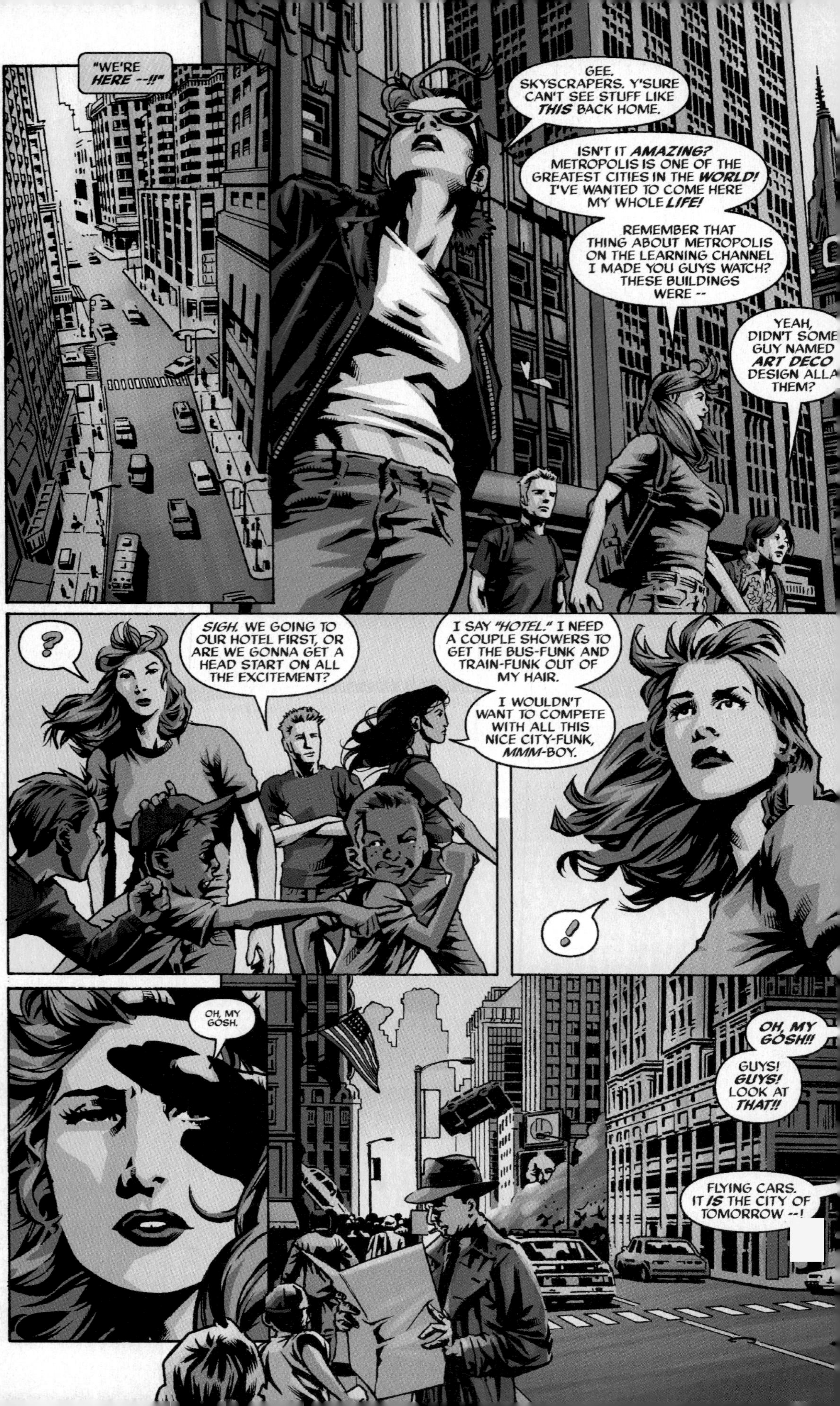
"WE'RE HERE --!!"
GEE. SKYSCRAPERS. Y'SURE CAN'T SEE STUFF LIKE THIS BACK HOME.
ISN'T IT AMAZING? METROPOLIS IS ONE OF THE GREATEST CITIES IN THE WORLD! I'VE WANTED TO COME HERE MY WHOLE LIFE!
REMEMBER THAT THING ABOUT METROPOLIS ON THE LEARNING CHANNEL I MADE YOU GUYS WATCH? THESE BUILDINGS WERE --
YEAH, DIDN'T SOME GUY NAMED ART DECO DESIGN ALLA THEM?
?
SIGH. WE GOING TO OUR HOTEL FIRST, OR ARE WE GONNA GET A HEAD START ON ALL THE EXCITEMENT?
I SAY "HOTEL." I NEED A COUPLE SHOWERS TO GET THE BUS-FUNK AND TRAIN-FUNK OUT OF MY HAIR.
I WOULDN'T WANT TO COMPETE WITH ALL THIS NICE CITY-FUNK, MMM-BOY.
!
OH, MY GOSH.
OH, MY GOSH!!
GUYS! GUYS! LOOK AT THAT!!
FLYING CARS. IT IS THE CITY OF TOMORROW --!

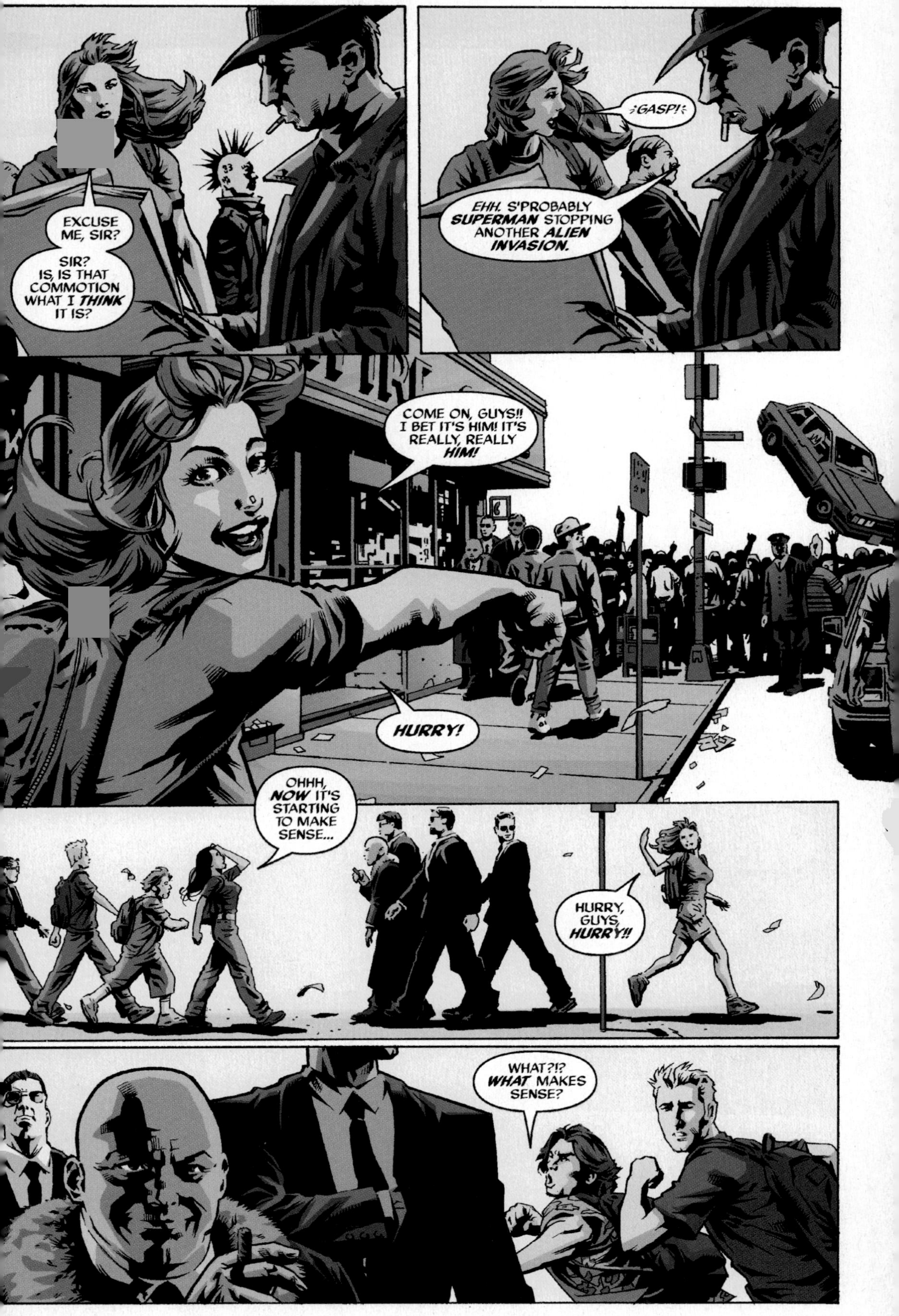
EXCUSE ME, SIR?
SIR? IS, IS THAT COMMOTION WHAT I THINK IT IS?
GASP!
EHH. S'PROBABLY SUPERMAN STOPPING ANOTHER ALIEN INVASION.
COME ON, GUYS!! I BET IT'S HIM! IT'S REALLY, REALLY HIM!
HURRY!
OHHH, NOW IT'S STARTING TO MAKE SENSE...
HURRY, GUYS, HURRY!!
WHAT?!? WHAT MAKES SENSE?

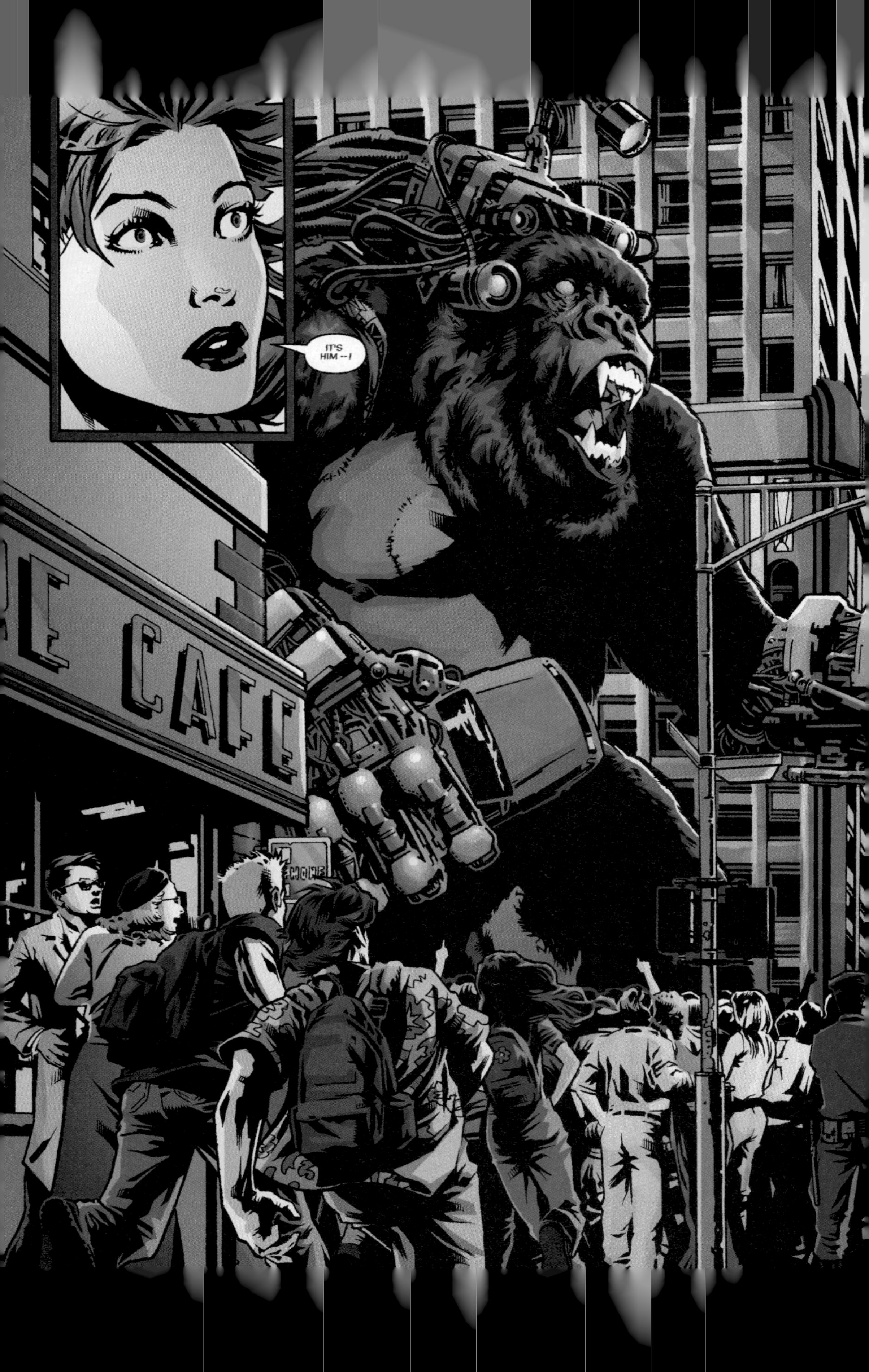
IT'S HIM --!
CAFE

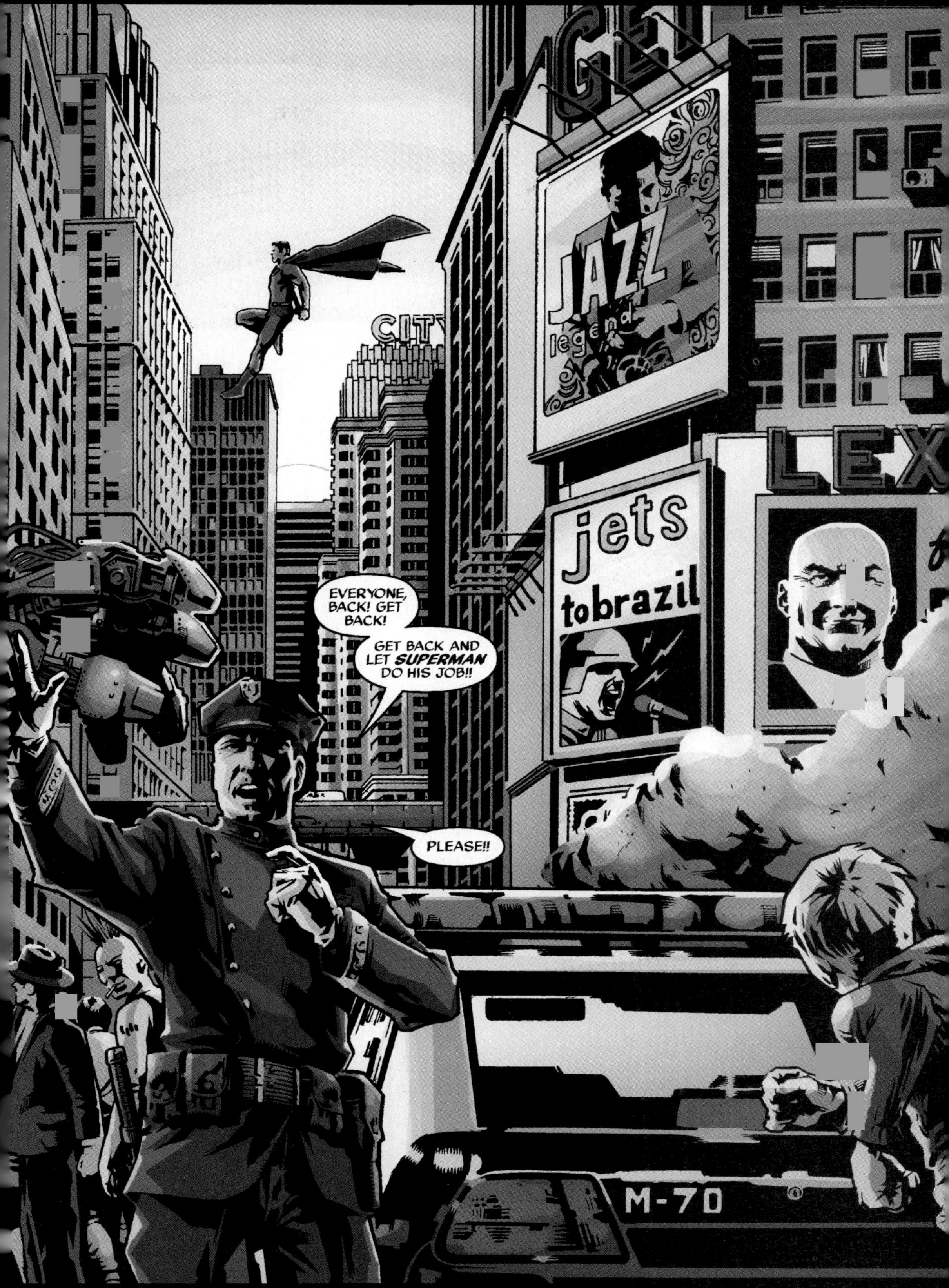

EVERYONE, BACK! GET BACK!
GET BACK AND LET SUPERMAN DO HIS JOB!!
PLEASE!!
JAZZ legend
jets tobrazil
LEX
CITY
M-70

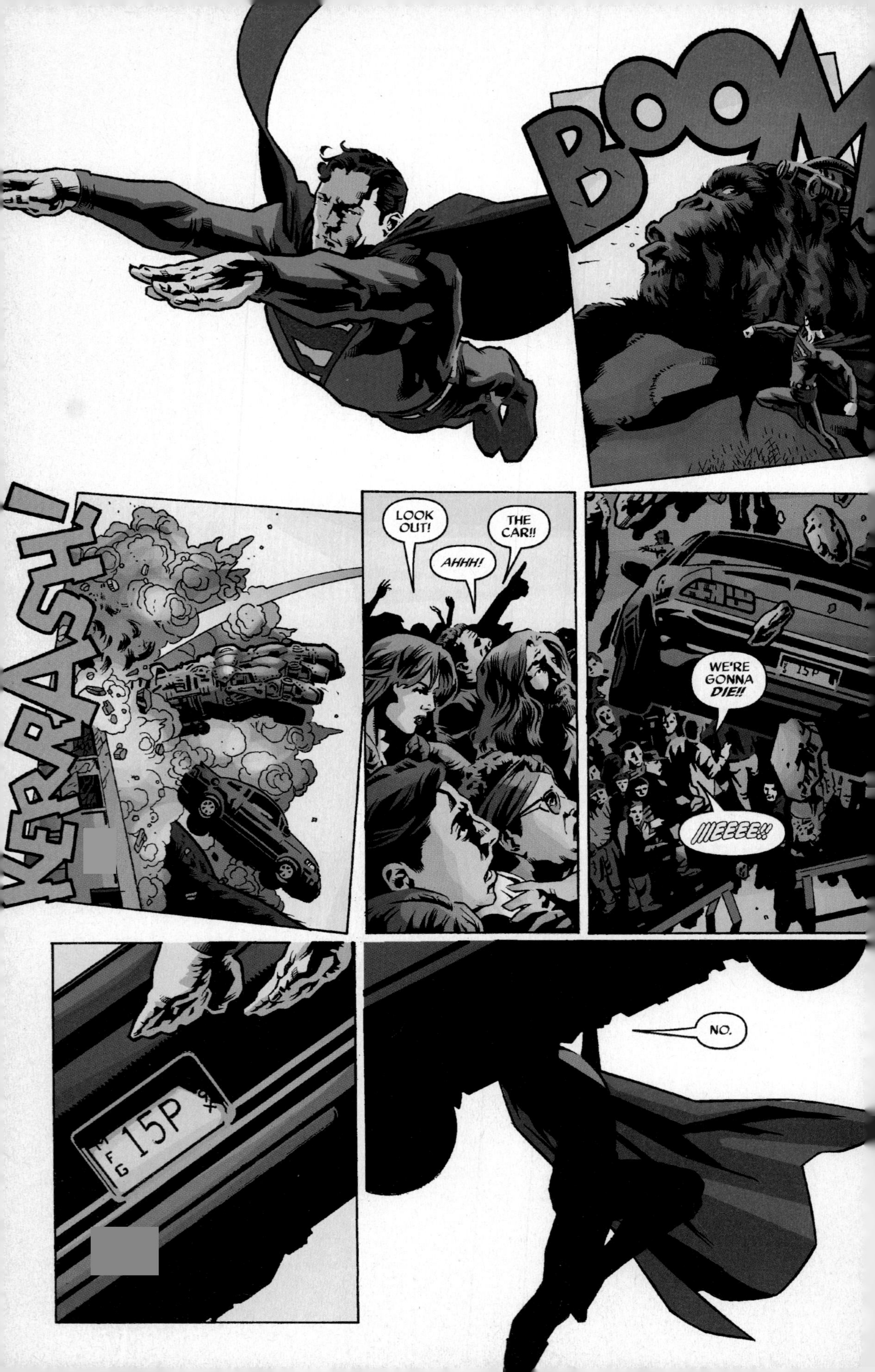
BOOM
KERASH!
LOOK OUT!
AHHH!
THE CAR!!
WE'RE GONNA DIE!!
IIIEEEEE!!
15P
NO.

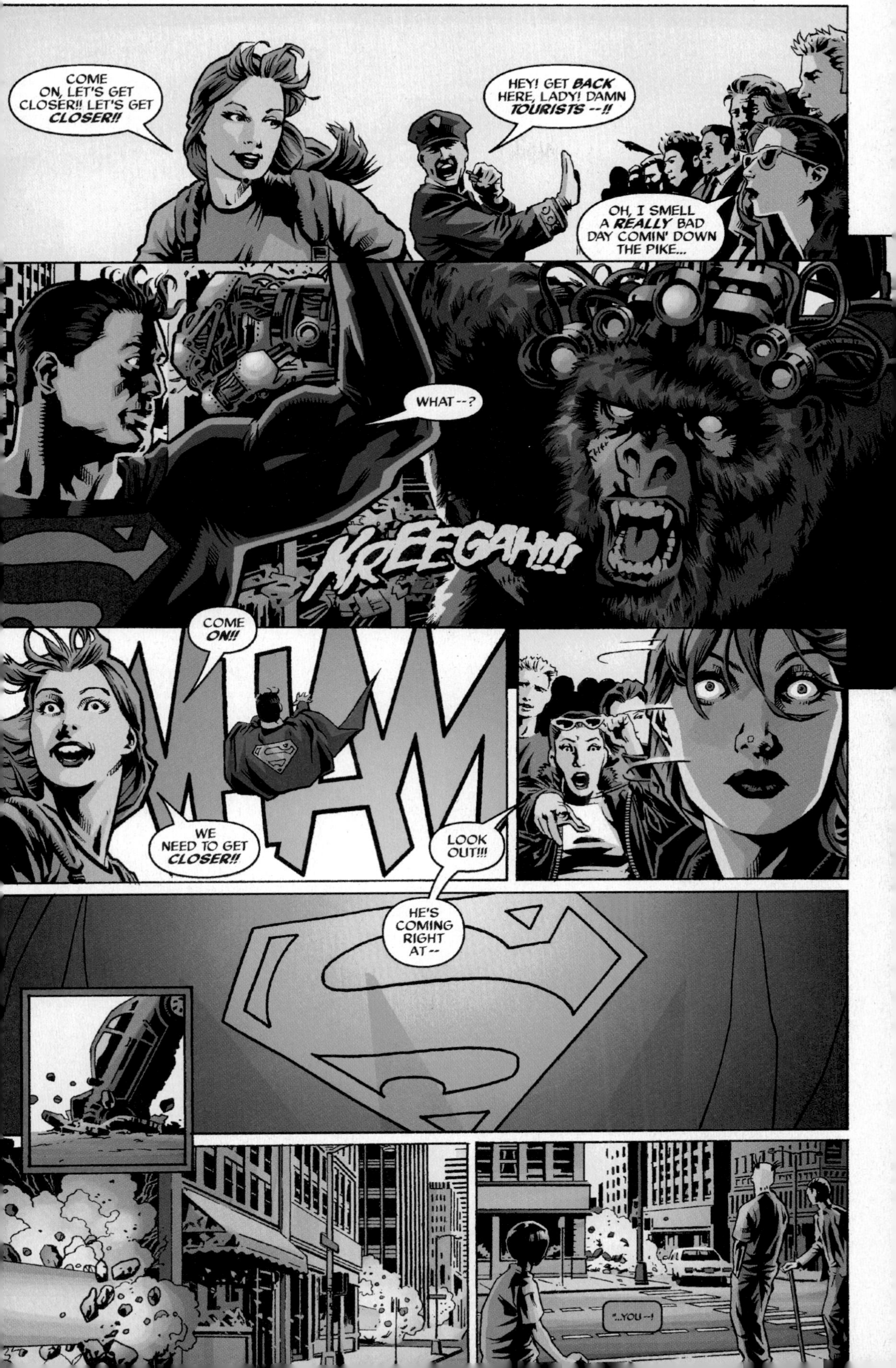
COME ON, LET'S GET CLOSER!! LET'S GET **CLOSER!!**
HEY! GET **BACK** HERE, LADY! DAMN **TOURISTS --!!**
OH, I SMELL A **REALLY** BAD DAY COMIN' DOWN THE PIKE...
WHAT--?
KREEGAH!!!
COME **ON!!**
WE NEED TO GET **CLOSER!!**
LOOK OUT!!!
HE'S COMING RIGHT AT--
"...YOU--!

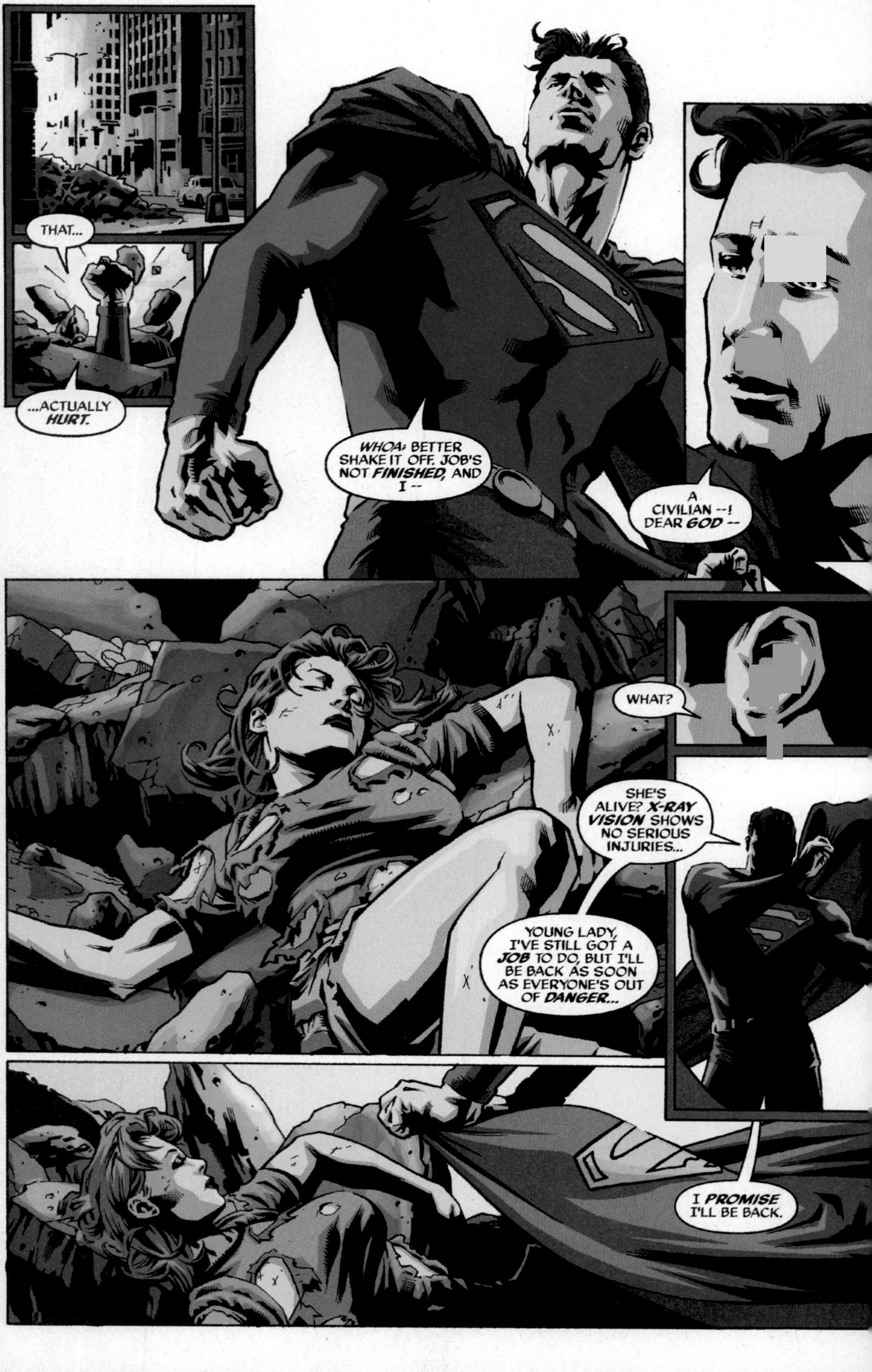

THAT...
...ACTUALLY HURT.
WHOA: BETTER SHAKE IT OFF. JOB'S NOT FINISHED, AND I --
A CIVILIAN --! DEAR GOD --
WHAT?
SHE'S ALIVE? X-RAY VISION SHOWS NO SERIOUS INJURIES...
YOUNG LADY, I'VE STILL GOT A JOB TO DO, BUT I'LL BE BACK AS SOON AS EVERYONE'S OUT OF DANGER...
I PROMISE I'LL BE BACK.

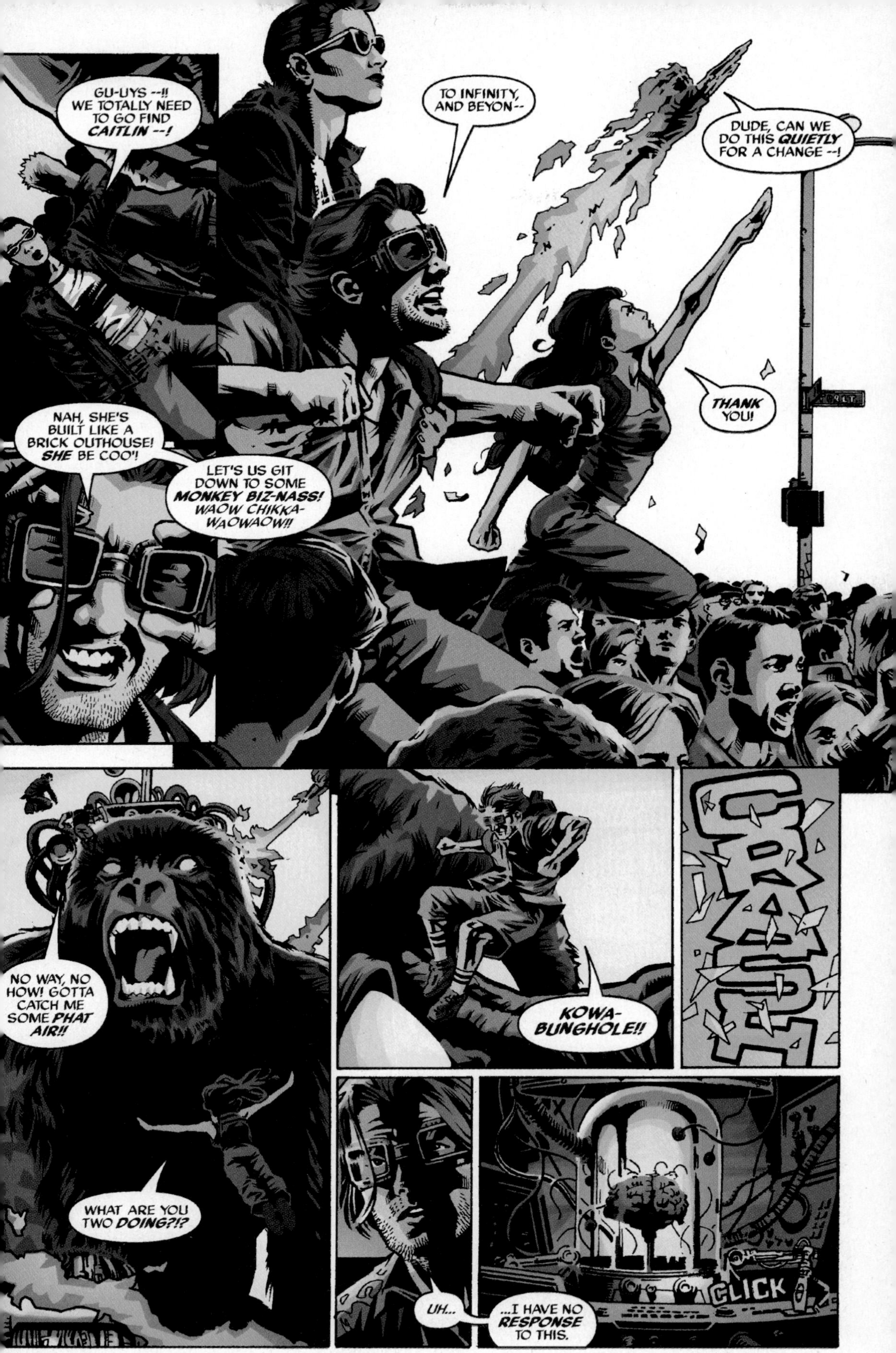
GU-UYS --!! WE TOTALLY NEED TO GO FIND CAITLIN --!
TO INFINITY, AND BEYON--
DUDE, CAN WE DO THIS QUIETLY FOR A CHANGE --!
THANK YOU!
NAH, SHE'S BUILT LIKE A BRICK OUTHOUSE! SHE BE COO'!
LET'S US GIT DOWN TO SOME MONKEY BIZ-NASS! WAOW CHIKKA-WAOWAOW!!
NO WAY, NO HOW! GOTTA CATCH ME SOME PHAT AIR!!
WHAT ARE YOU TWO DOING?!?
KOWA-BUNGHOLE!!
CRASH
CLICK
UH...
...I HAVE NO RESPONSE TO THIS.

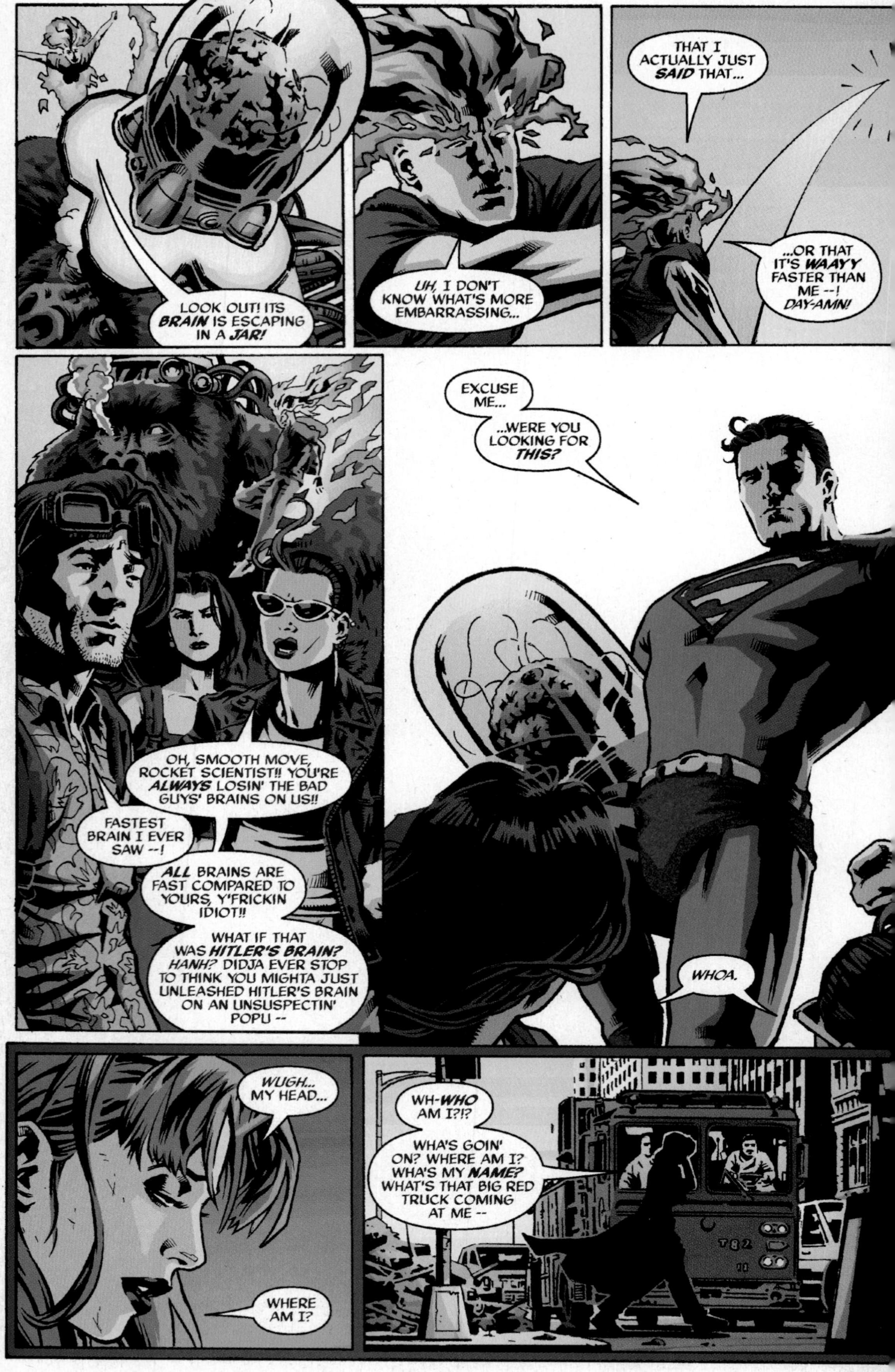
LOOK OUT! ITS BRAIN IS ESCAPING IN A JAR!
UH, I DON'T KNOW WHAT'S MORE EMBARRASSING...
THAT I ACTUALLY JUST SAID THAT...
...OR THAT IT'S WAAY'Y FASTER THAN ME --! DAY-AMN!
OH, SMOOTH MOVE, ROCKET SCIENTIST!! YOU'RE ALWAYS LOSIN' THE BAD GUYS' BRAINS ON US!!
FASTEST BRAIN I EVER SAW --!
ALL BRAINS ARE FAST COMPARED TO YOURS, Y'FRICKIN IDIOT!!
WHAT IF THAT WAS HITLER'S BRAIN? HANH? DIDJA EVER STOP TO THINK YOU MIGHTA JUST UNLEASHED HITLER'S BRAIN ON AN UNSUSPECTIN' POPU --
EXCUSE ME...
...WERE YOU LOOKING FOR THIS?
WHOA.
WUGH... MY HEAD...
WHERE AM I?
WH-WHO AM I?!?
WHA'S GOIN' ON? WHERE AM I? WHA'S MY NAME? WHAT'S THAT BIG RED TRUCK COMING AT ME --

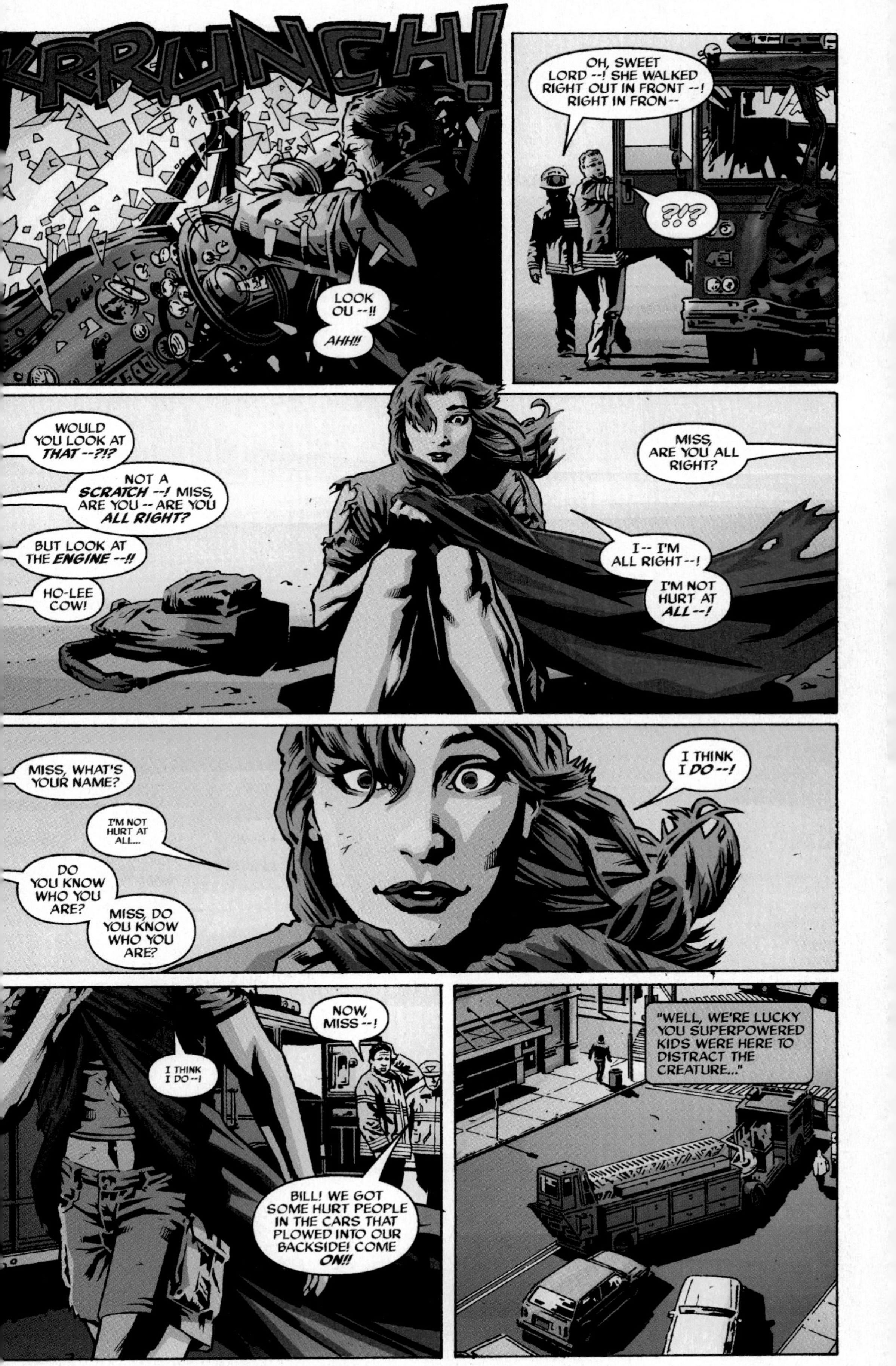
KRRUNCH!
LOOK OU --!!
AHH!!
OH, SWEET LORD --! SHE WALKED RIGHT OUT IN FRONT --! RIGHT IN FRON--
?!?
WOULD YOU LOOK AT THAT --?!?
NOT A SCRATCH --! MISS, ARE YOU -- ARE YOU ALL RIGHT?
BUT LOOK AT THE ENGINE --!!
HO-LEE COW!
MISS, ARE YOU ALL RIGHT?
I-- I'M ALL RIGHT --!
I'M NOT HURT AT ALL --!
MISS, WHAT'S YOUR NAME?
I'M NOT HURT AT ALL...
DO YOU KNOW WHO YOU ARE?
MISS, DO YOU KNOW WHO YOU ARE?
I THINK I DO --!
I THINK I DO --!
NOW, MISS --!
BILL! WE GOT SOME HURT PEOPLE IN THE CARS THAT PLOWED INTO OUR BACKSIDE! COME ON!!
"WELL, WE'RE LUCKY YOU SUPERPOWERED KIDS WERE HERE TO DISTRACT THE CREATURE..."

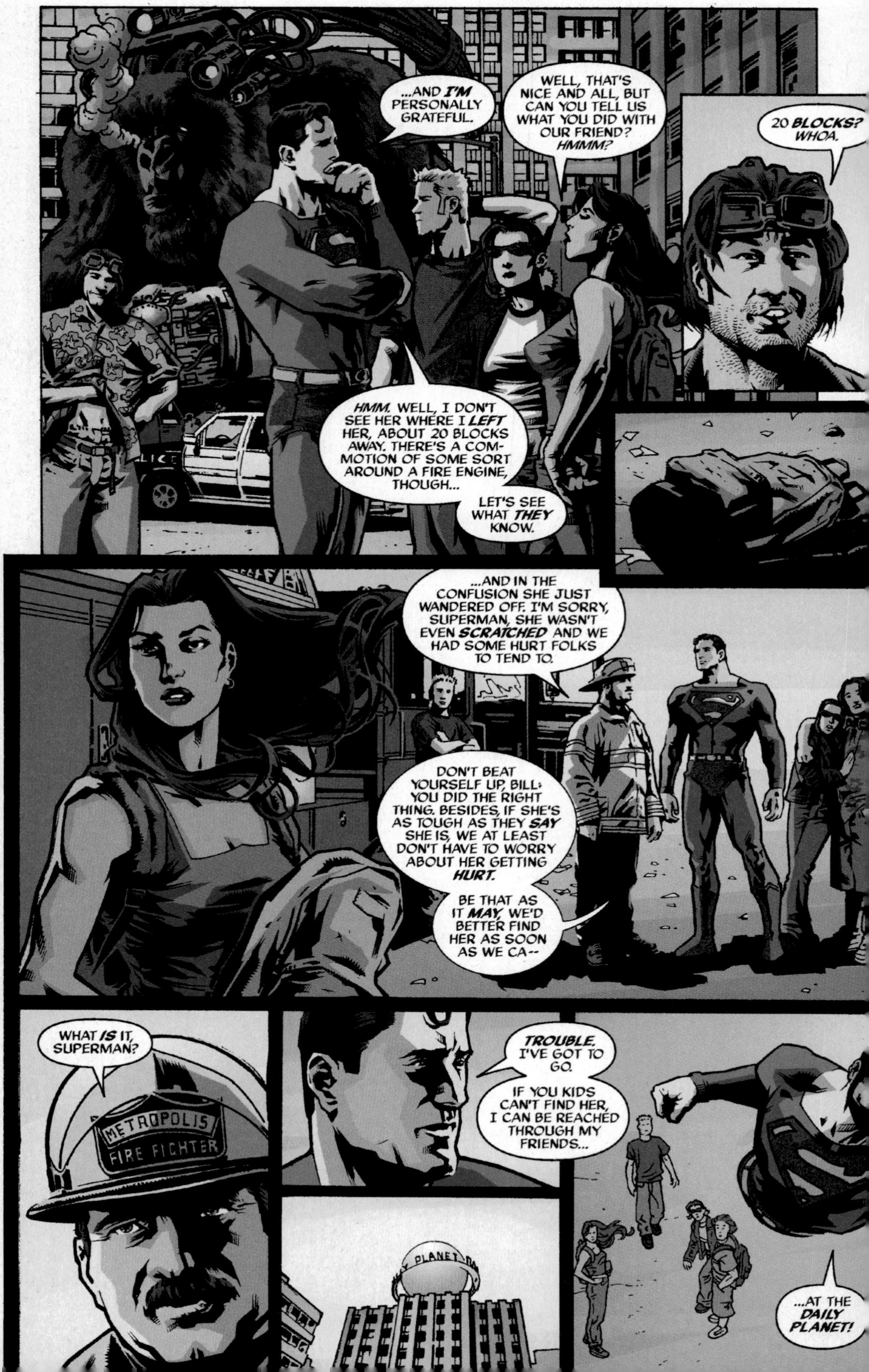
...AND I'M PERSONALLY GRATEFUL.
WELL, THAT'S NICE AND ALL, BUT CAN YOU TELL US WHAT YOU DID WITH OUR FRIEND? HMMM?
HMM. WELL, I DON'T SEE HER WHERE I LEFT HER, ABOUT 20 BLOCKS AWAY. THERE'S A COMMOTION OF SOME SORT AROUND A FIRE ENGINE, THOUGH...
LET'S SEE WHAT THEY KNOW.
20 BLOCKS? WHOA.
...AND IN THE CONFUSION SHE JUST WANDERED OFF. I'M SORRY, SUPERMAN, SHE WASN'T EVEN SCRATCHED AND WE HAD SOME HURT FOLKS TO TEND TO.
DON'T BEAT YOURSELF UP, BILL; YOU DID THE RIGHT THING. BESIDES, IF SHE'S AS TOUGH AS THEY SAY SHE IS, WE AT LEAST DON'T HAVE TO WORRY ABOUT HER GETTING HURT.
BE THAT AS IT MAY, WE'D BETTER FIND HER AS SOON AS WE CA--
WHAT IS IT, SUPERMAN?
METROPOLIS
FIRE FIGHTER
TROUBLE. I'VE GOT TO GO.
IF YOU KIDS CAN'T FIND HER, I CAN BE REACHED THROUGH MY FRIENDS...
...AT THE DAILY PLANET!

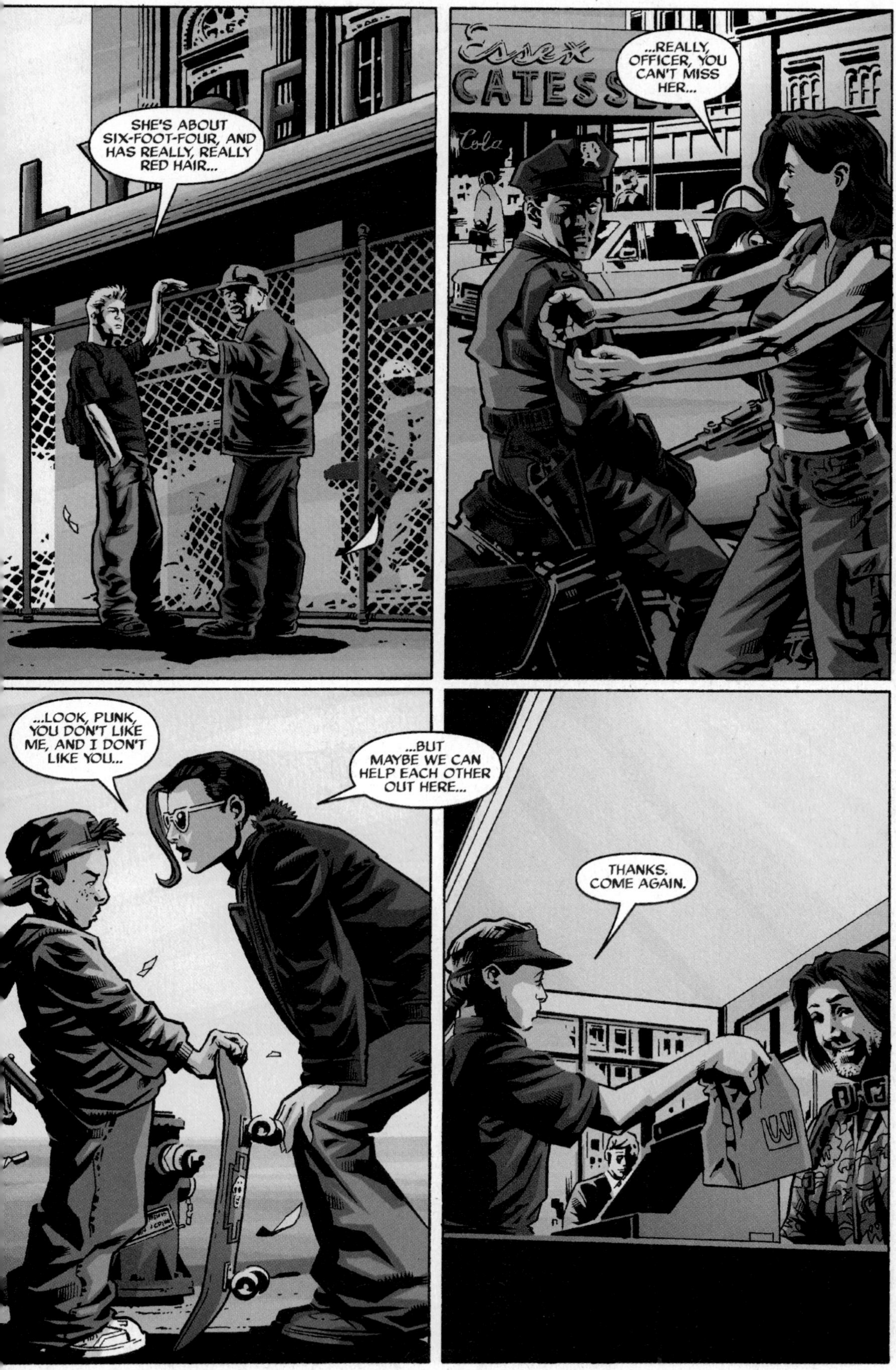
SHE'S ABOUT SIX-FOOT-FOUR, AND HAS REALLY, REALLY RED HAIR...
...REALLY, OFFICER, YOU CAN'T MISS HER...
...LOOK, PUNK, YOU DON'T LIKE ME, AND I DON'T LIKE YOU...
...BUT MAYBE WE CAN HELP EACH OTHER OUT HERE...
THANKS. COME AGAIN.

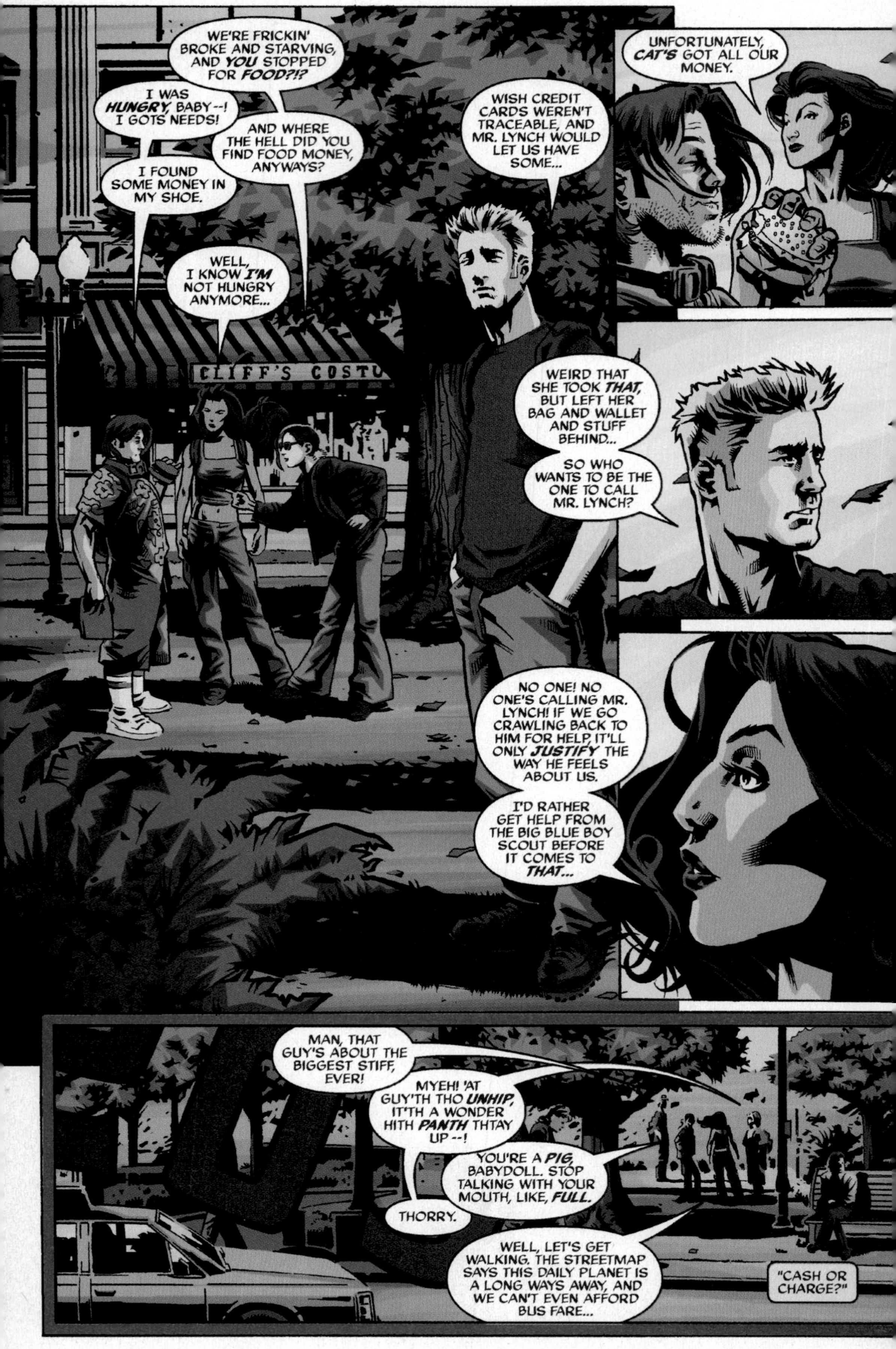
WE'RE FRICKIN' BROKE AND STARVING, AND YOU STOPPED FOR FOOD?!?
I WAS HUNGRY, BABY--! I GOTS NEEDS!
AND WHERE THE HELL DID YOU FIND FOOD MONEY, ANYWAYS?
I FOUND SOME MONEY IN MY SHOE.
WELL, I KNOW I'M NOT HUNGRY ANYMORE...
CLIFF'S COSTU
WISH CREDIT CARDS WEREN'T TRACEABLE, AND MR. LYNCH WOULD LET US HAVE SOME...
UNFORTUNATELY, CAT'S GOT ALL OUR MONEY.
WEIRD THAT SHE TOOK THAT, BUT LEFT HER BAG AND WALLET AND STUFF BEHIND...
SO WHO WANTS TO BE THE ONE TO CALL MR. LYNCH?
NO ONE! NO ONE'S CALLING MR. LYNCH! IF WE GO CRAWLING BACK TO HIM FOR HELP, IT'LL ONLY JUSTIFY THE WAY HE FEELS ABOUT US.
I'D RATHER GET HELP FROM THE BIG BLUE BOY SCOUT BEFORE IT COMES TO THAT...
MAN, THAT GUY'S ABOUT THE BIGGEST STIFF, EVER!
MYEH! 'AT GUY'TH THO UNHIP, IT'TH A WONDER HITH PANTH THTAY UP--!
YOU'RE A PIG, BABYDOLL. STOP TALKING WITH YOUR MOUTH, LIKE, FULL.
THORRY.
WELL, LET'S GET WALKING. THE STREETMAP SAYS THIS DAILY PLANET IS A LONG WAYS AWAY, AND WE CAN'T EVEN AFFORD BUS FARE...
"CASH OR CHARGE?"

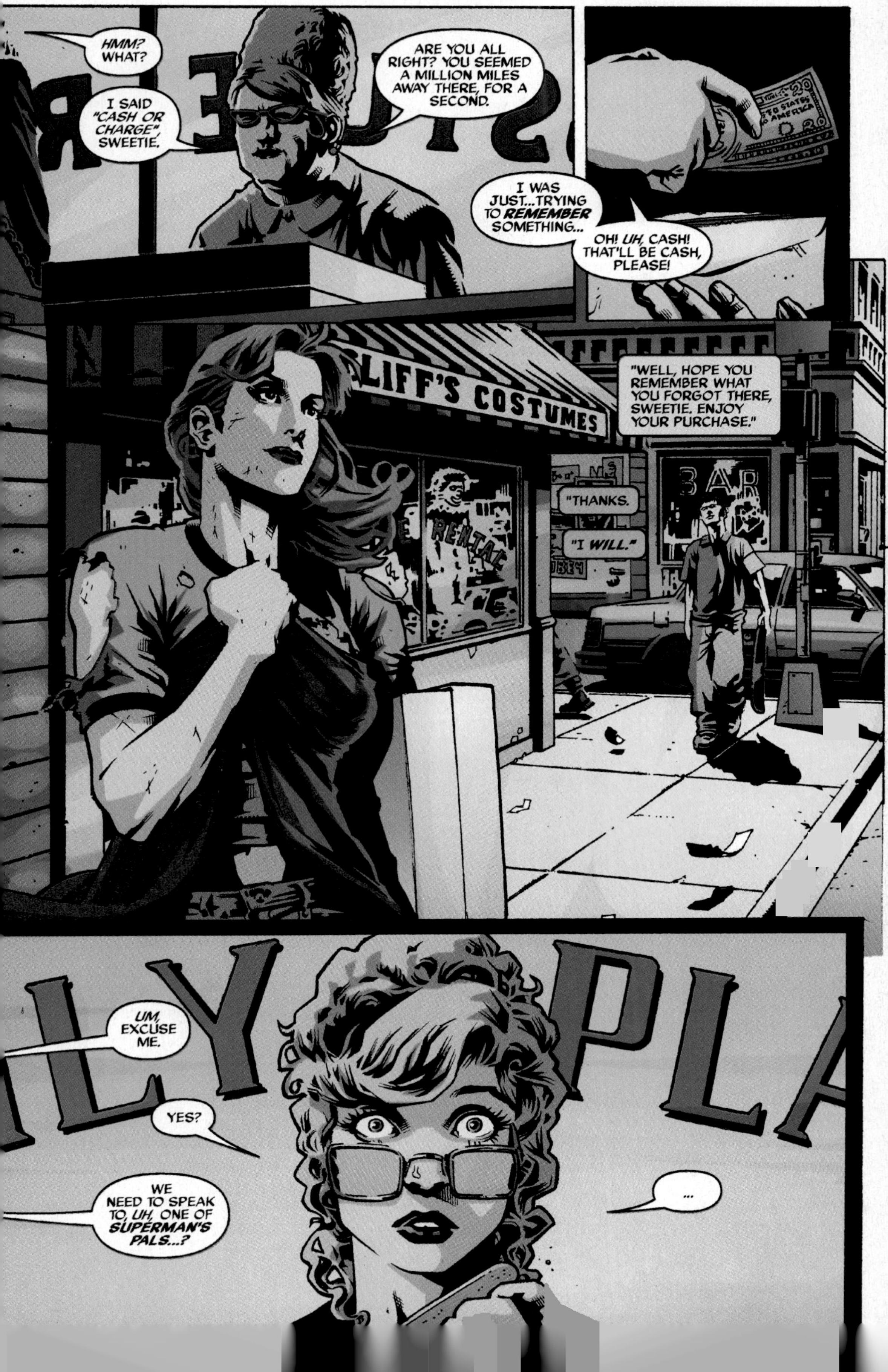

HMM? WHAT?
ARE YOU ALL RIGHT? YOU SEEMED A MILLION MILES AWAY THERE, FOR A SECOND.
I SAID "CASH OR CHARGE", SWEETIE.
I WAS JUST...TRYING TO REMEMBER SOMETHING...
OH! UH, CASH! THAT'LL BE CASH, PLEASE!
CLIFF'S COSTUMES
RENTAL
"WELL, HOPE YOU REMEMBER WHAT YOU FORGOT THERE, SWEETIE. ENJOY YOUR PURCHASE."
"THANKS.
"I WILL."
BAR
UM, EXCUSE ME.
YES?
WE NEED TO SPEAK TO, UH, ONE OF SUPERMAN'S PALS...?
...

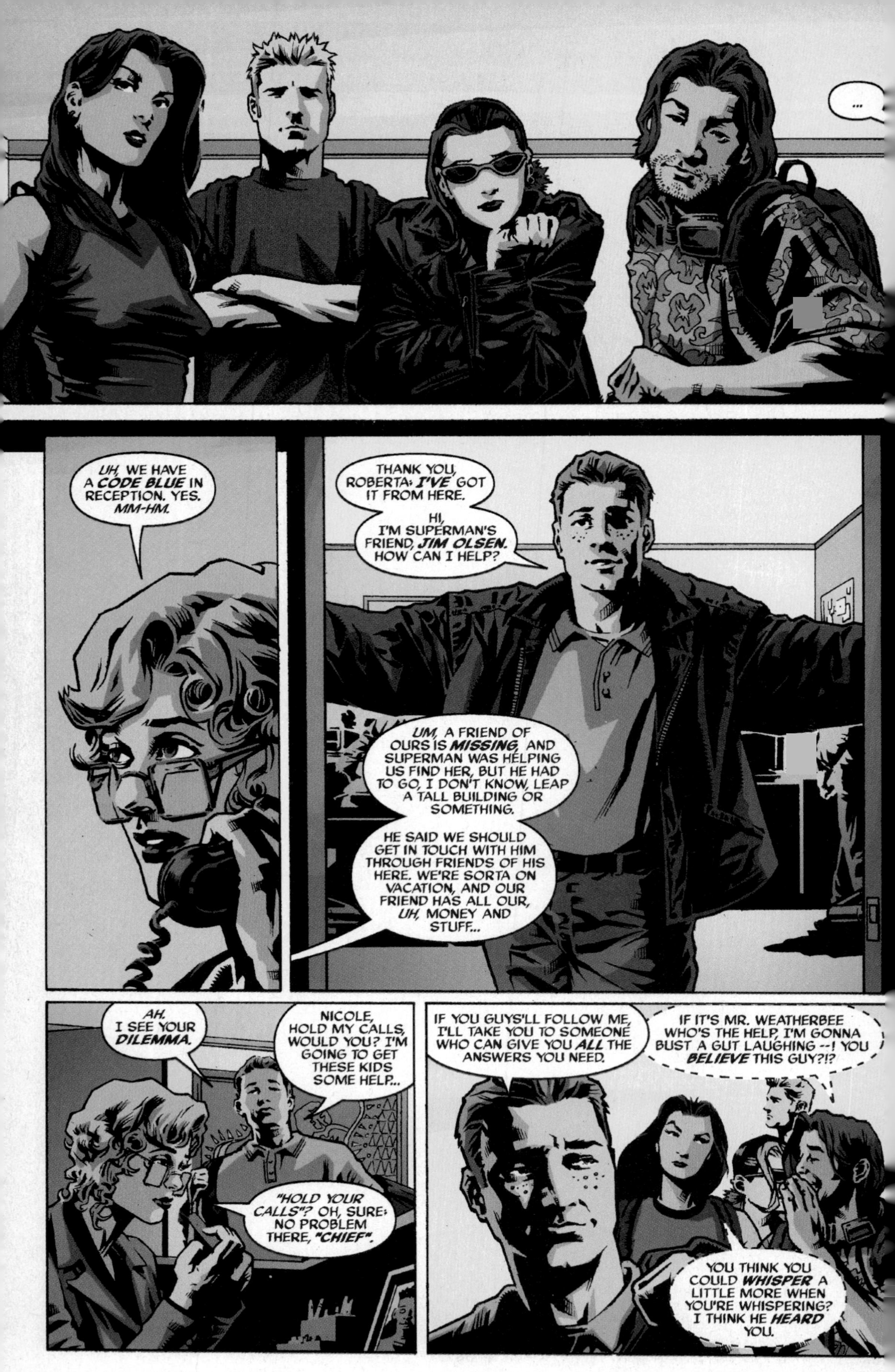
...
UH, WE HAVE A CODE BLUE IN RECEPTION. YES. MM-HM.
THANK YOU, ROBERTA; I'VE GOT IT FROM HERE.
HI, I'M SUPERMAN'S FRIEND, JIM OLSEN. HOW CAN I HELP?
UM, A FRIEND OF OURS IS MISSING, AND SUPERMAN WAS HELPING US FIND HER, BUT HE HAD TO GO, I DON'T KNOW, LEAP A TALL BUILDING OR SOMETHING.
HE SAID WE SHOULD GET IN TOUCH WITH HIM THROUGH FRIENDS OF HIS HERE. WE'RE SORTA ON VACATION, AND OUR FRIEND HAS ALL OUR, UH, MONEY AND STUFF...
AH. I SEE YOUR DILEMMA.
NICOLE, HOLD MY CALLS, WOULD YOU? I'M GOING TO GET THESE KIDS SOME HELP...
"HOLD YOUR CALLS"? OH, SURE; NO PROBLEM THERE, "CHIEF".
IF YOU GUYS'LL FOLLOW ME, I'LL TAKE YOU TO SOMEONE WHO CAN GIVE YOU ALL THE ANSWERS YOU NEED.
IF IT'S MR. WEATHERBEE WHO'S THE HELP, I'M GONNA BUST A GUT LAUGHING --! YOU BELIEVE THIS GUY?!?
YOU THINK YOU COULD WHISPER A LITTLE MORE WHEN YOU'RE WHISPERING? I THINK HE HEARD YOU.

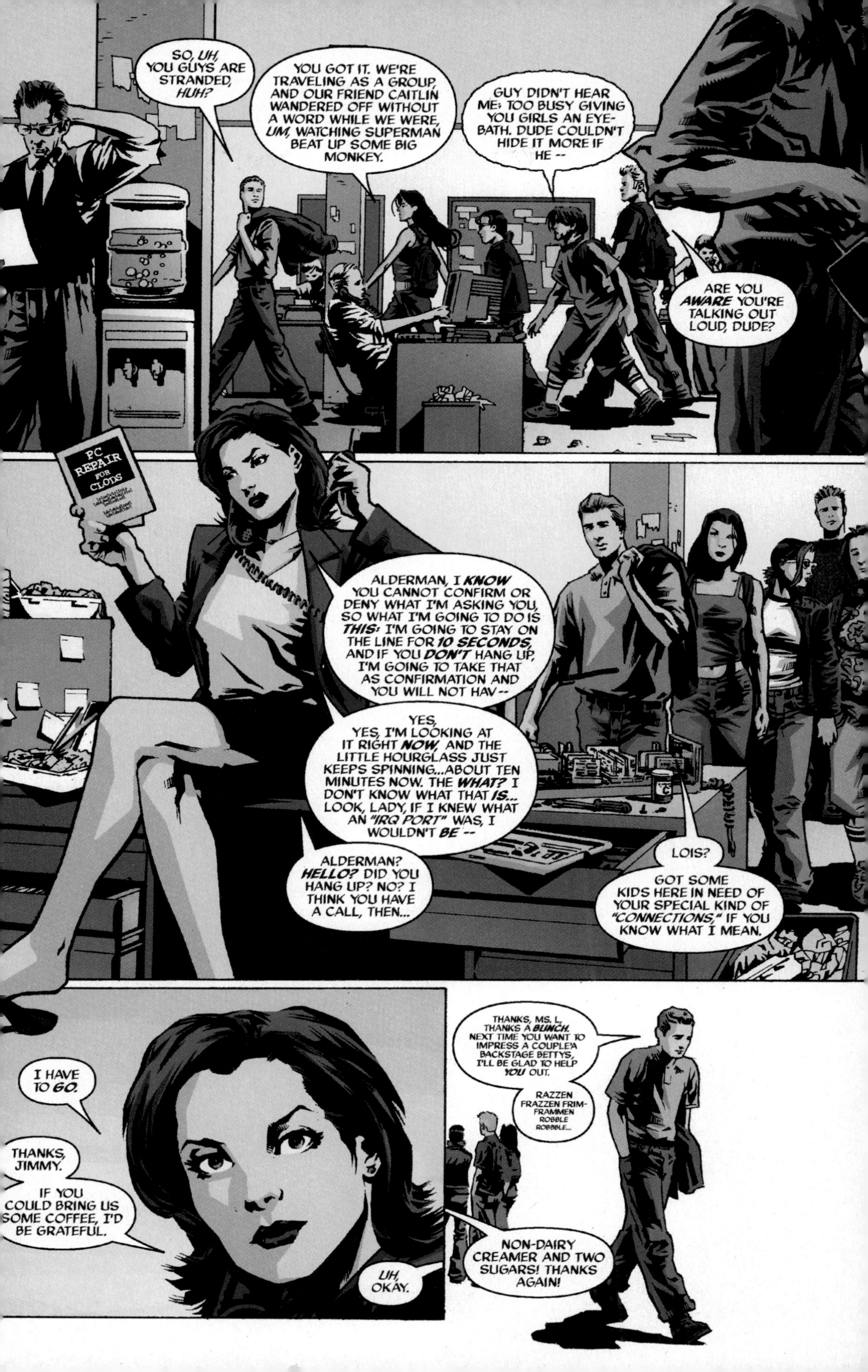
SO, UH, YOU GUYS ARE STRANDED, HUH?
YOU GOT IT. WE'RE TRAVELING AS A GROUP, AND OUR FRIEND CAITLIN WANDERED OFF WITHOUT A WORD WHILE WE WERE, UM, WATCHING SUPERMAN BEAT UP SOME BIG MONKEY.
GUY DIDN'T HEAR ME; TOO BUSY GIVING YOU GIRLS AN EYE-BATH. DUDE COULDN'T HIDE IT MORE IF HE --
ARE YOU AWARE YOU'RE TALKING OUT LOUD, DUDE?
PC REPAIR FOR CLODS
ALDERMAN, I KNOW YOU CANNOT CONFIRM OR DENY WHAT I'M ASKING YOU, SO WHAT I'M GOING TO DO IS THIS: I'M GOING TO STAY ON THE LINE FOR 10 SECONDS, AND IF YOU DON'T HANG UP, I'M GOING TO TAKE THAT AS CONFIRMATION AND YOU WILL NOT HAV --
YES, YES, I'M LOOKING AT IT RIGHT NOW, AND THE LITTLE HOURGLASS JUST KEEPS SPINNING...ABOUT TEN MINUTES NOW. THE WHAT? I DON'T KNOW WHAT THAT IS... LOOK, LADY, IF I KNEW WHAT AN "IRQ PORT" WAS, I WOULDN'T BE --
ALDERMAN? HELLO? DID YOU HANG UP? NO? I THINK YOU HAVE A CALL, THEN...
LOIS?
GOT SOME KIDS HERE IN NEED OF YOUR SPECIAL KIND OF "CONNECTIONS," IF YOU KNOW WHAT I MEAN.
I HAVE TO GO.
THANKS, JIMMY.
IF YOU COULD BRING US SOME COFFEE, I'D BE GRATEFUL.
UH, OKAY.
THANKS, MS. L. THANKS A BUNCH. NEXT TIME YOU WANT TO IMPRESS A COUPLE'A BACKSTAGE BETTYS, I'LL BE GLAD TO HELP YOU OUT.
RAZZEN FRAZZEN FRIM-FRAMMEN ROBBLE ROBBLE...
NON-DAIRY CREAMER AND TWO SUGARS! THANKS AGAIN!

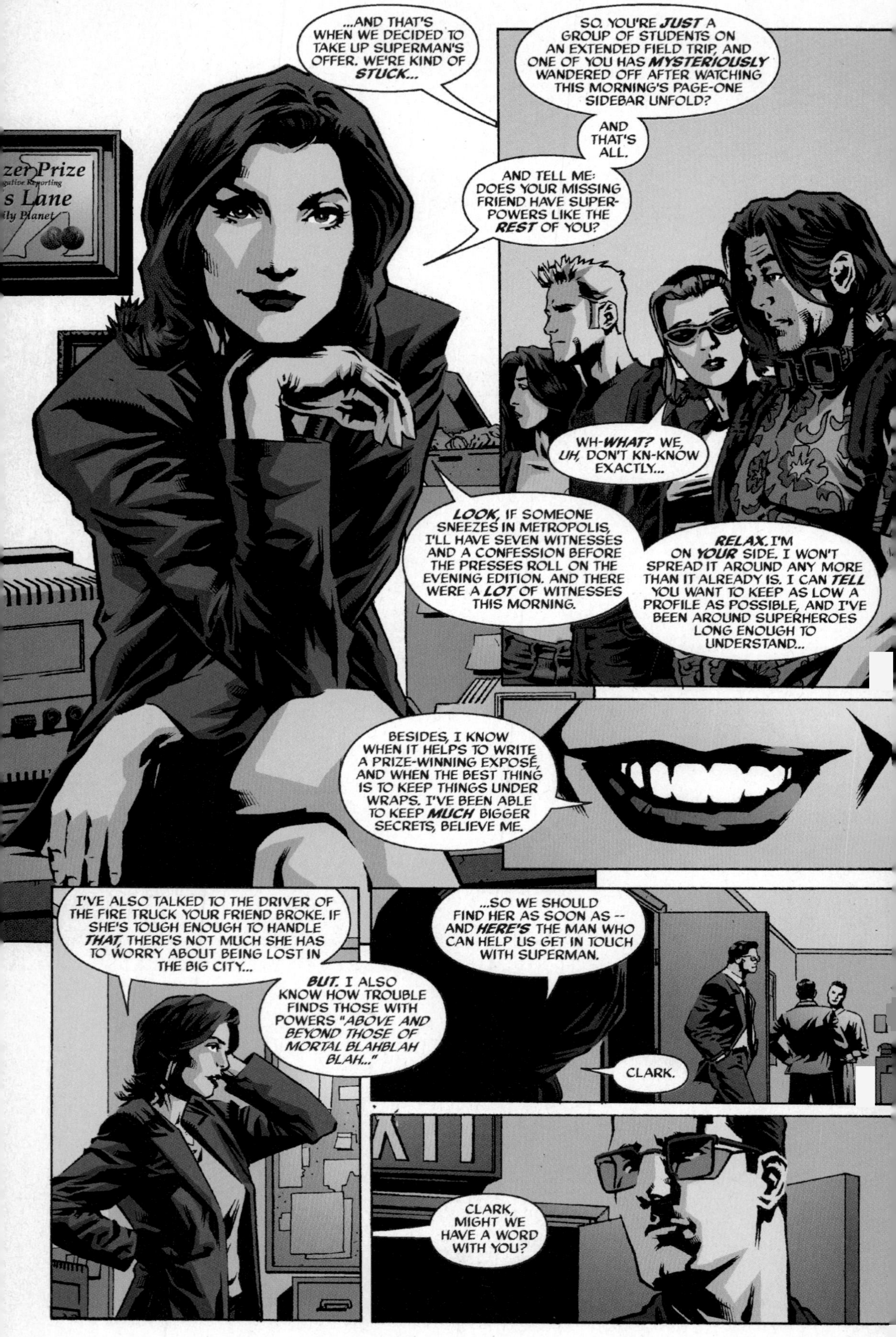

...AND THAT'S WHEN WE DECIDED TO TAKE UP SUPERMAN'S OFFER. WE'RE KIND OF STUCK...
SO. YOU'RE JUST A GROUP OF STUDENTS ON AN EXTENDED FIELD TRIP, AND ONE OF YOU HAS MYSTERIOUSLY WANDERED OFF AFTER WATCHING THIS MORNING'S PAGE-ONE SIDEBAR UNFOLD?
AND THAT'S ALL.
AND TELL ME: DOES YOUR MISSING FRIEND HAVE SUPER-POWERS LIKE THE REST OF YOU?
zer Prize
s Lane
WH-WHAT? WE, UH, DON'T KN-KNOW EXACTLY...
LOOK, IF SOMEONE SNEEZES IN METROPOLIS, I'LL HAVE SEVEN WITNESSES AND A CONFESSION BEFORE THE PRESSES ROLL ON THE EVENING EDITION. AND THERE WERE A LOT OF WITNESSES THIS MORNING.
RELAX. I'M ON YOUR SIDE. I WON'T SPREAD IT AROUND ANY MORE THAN IT ALREADY IS. I CAN TELL YOU WANT TO KEEP AS LOW A PROFILE AS POSSIBLE, AND I'VE BEEN AROUND SUPERHEROES LONG ENOUGH TO UNDERSTAND...
BESIDES, I KNOW WHEN IT HELPS TO WRITE A PRIZE-WINNING EXPOSÉ, AND WHEN THE BEST THING IS TO KEEP THINGS UNDER WRAPS. I'VE BEEN ABLE TO KEEP MUCH BIGGER SECRETS, BELIEVE ME.
I'VE ALSO TALKED TO THE DRIVER OF THE FIRE TRUCK YOUR FRIEND BROKE. IF SHE'S TOUGH ENOUGH TO HANDLE THAT, THERE'S NOT MUCH SHE HAS TO WORRY ABOUT BEING LOST IN THE BIG CITY...
BUT. I ALSO KNOW HOW TROUBLE FINDS THOSE WITH POWERS "ABOVE AND BEYOND THOSE OF MORTAL BLAHBLAH BLAH..."
...SO WE SHOULD FIND HER AS SOON AS -- AND HERE'S THE MAN WHO CAN HELP US GET IN TOUCH WITH SUPERMAN.
CLARK.
CLARK, MIGHT WE HAVE A WORD WITH YOU?

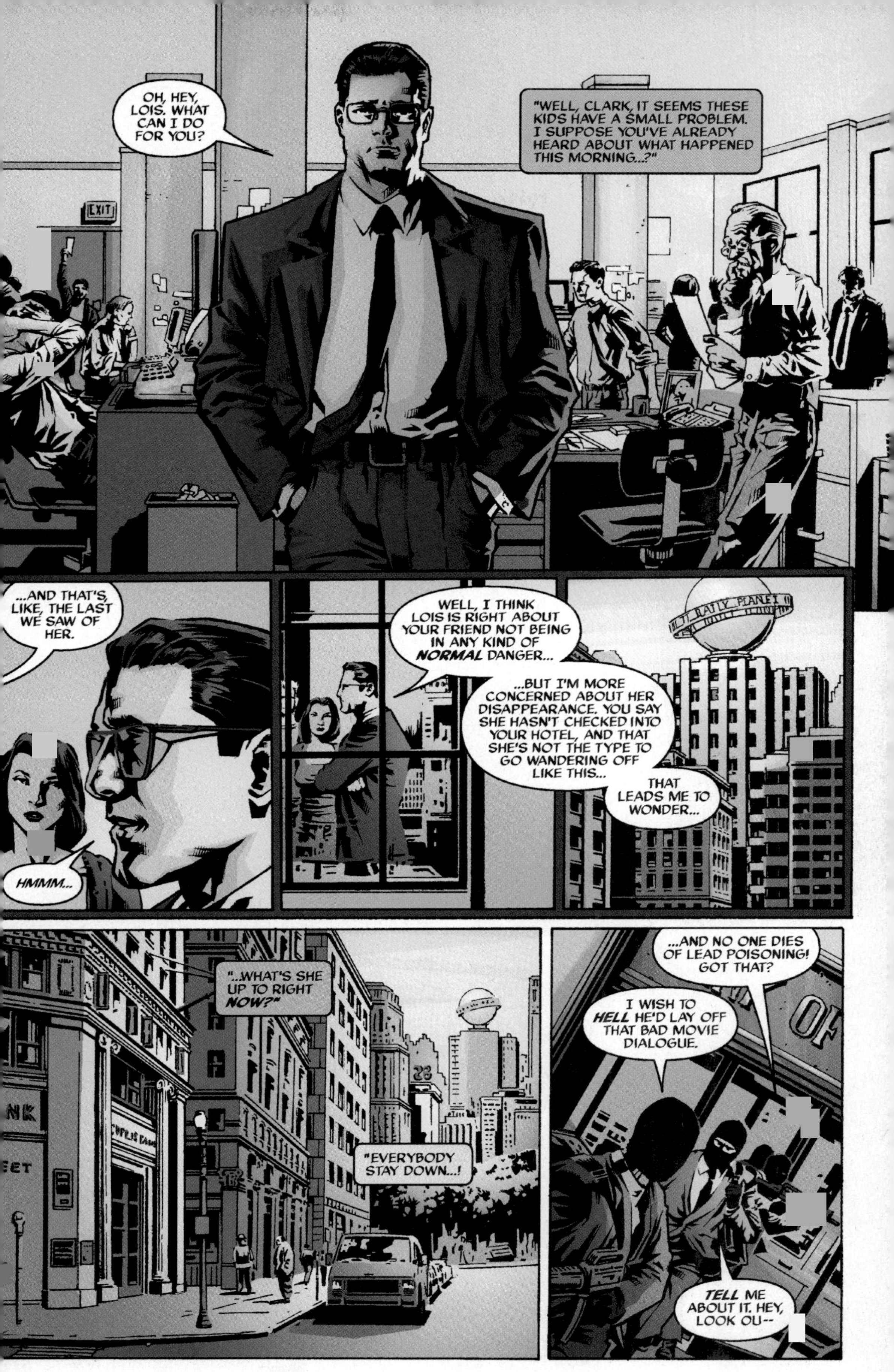
OH, HEY, LOIS. WHAT CAN I DO FOR YOU?
"WELL, CLARK, IT SEEMS THESE KIDS HAVE A SMALL PROBLEM. I SUPPOSE YOU'VE ALREADY HEARD ABOUT WHAT HAPPENED THIS MORNING...?"
EXIT
...AND THAT'S, LIKE, THE LAST WE SAW OF HER.
HMMM...
WELL, I THINK LOIS IS RIGHT ABOUT YOUR FRIEND NOT BEING IN ANY KIND OF *NORMAL* DANGER...
...BUT I'M MORE CONCERNED ABOUT HER DISAPPEARANCE. YOU SAY SHE HASN'T CHECKED INTO YOUR HOTEL, AND THAT SHE'S NOT THE TYPE TO GO WANDERING OFF LIKE THIS...
THAT LEADS ME TO WONDER...
"...WHAT'S SHE UP TO RIGHT *NOW?*"
"EVERYBODY STAY DOWN...!
...AND NO ONE DIES OF LEAD POISONING! GOT THAT?
I WISH TO *HELL* HE'D LAY OFF THAT BAD MOVIE DIALOGUE.
TELL ME ABOUT IT. HEY, LOOK OU--

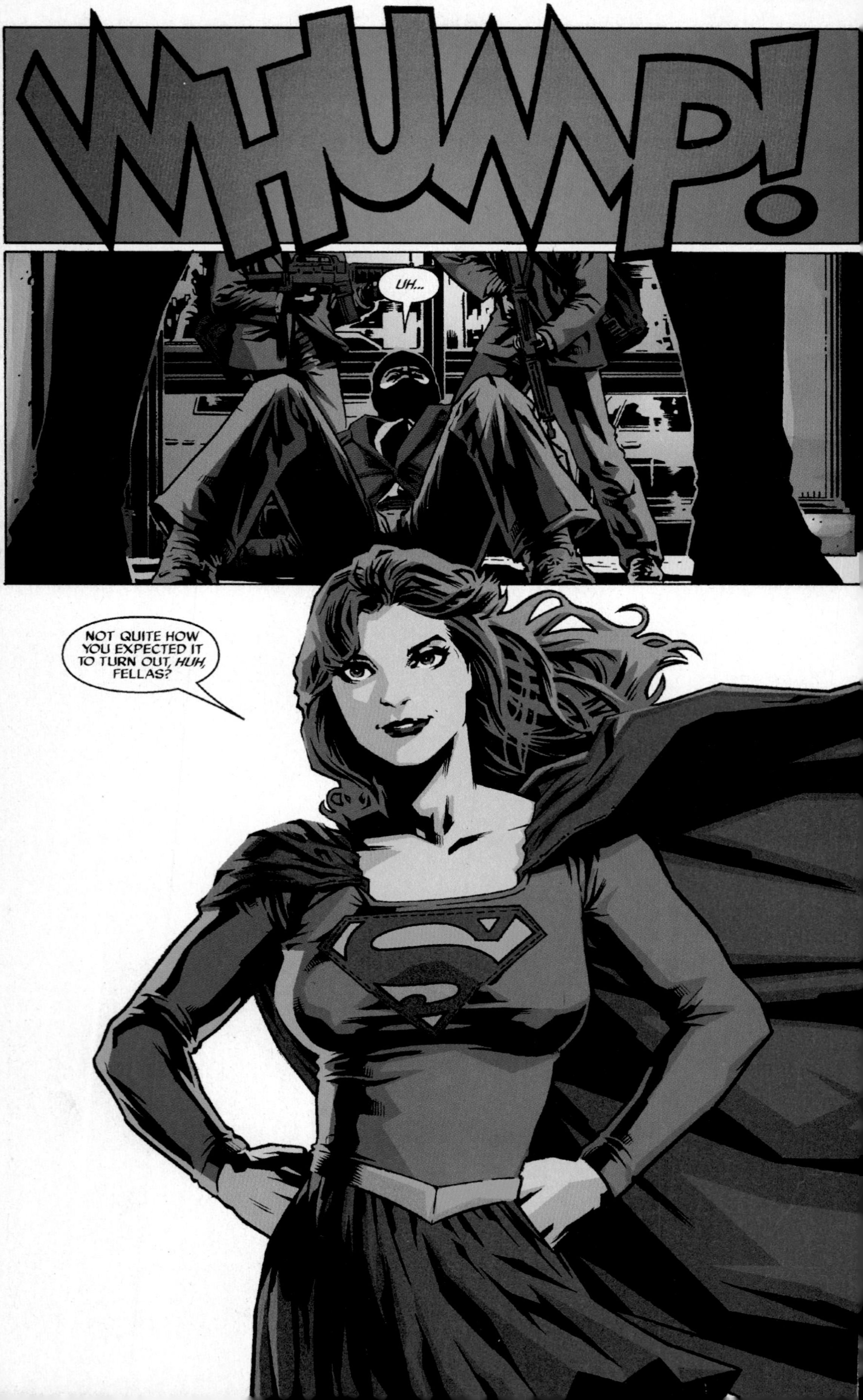
WHUMP!
UH...
NOT QUITE HOW YOU EXPECTED IT TO TURN OUT, *HUH,* FELLAS?

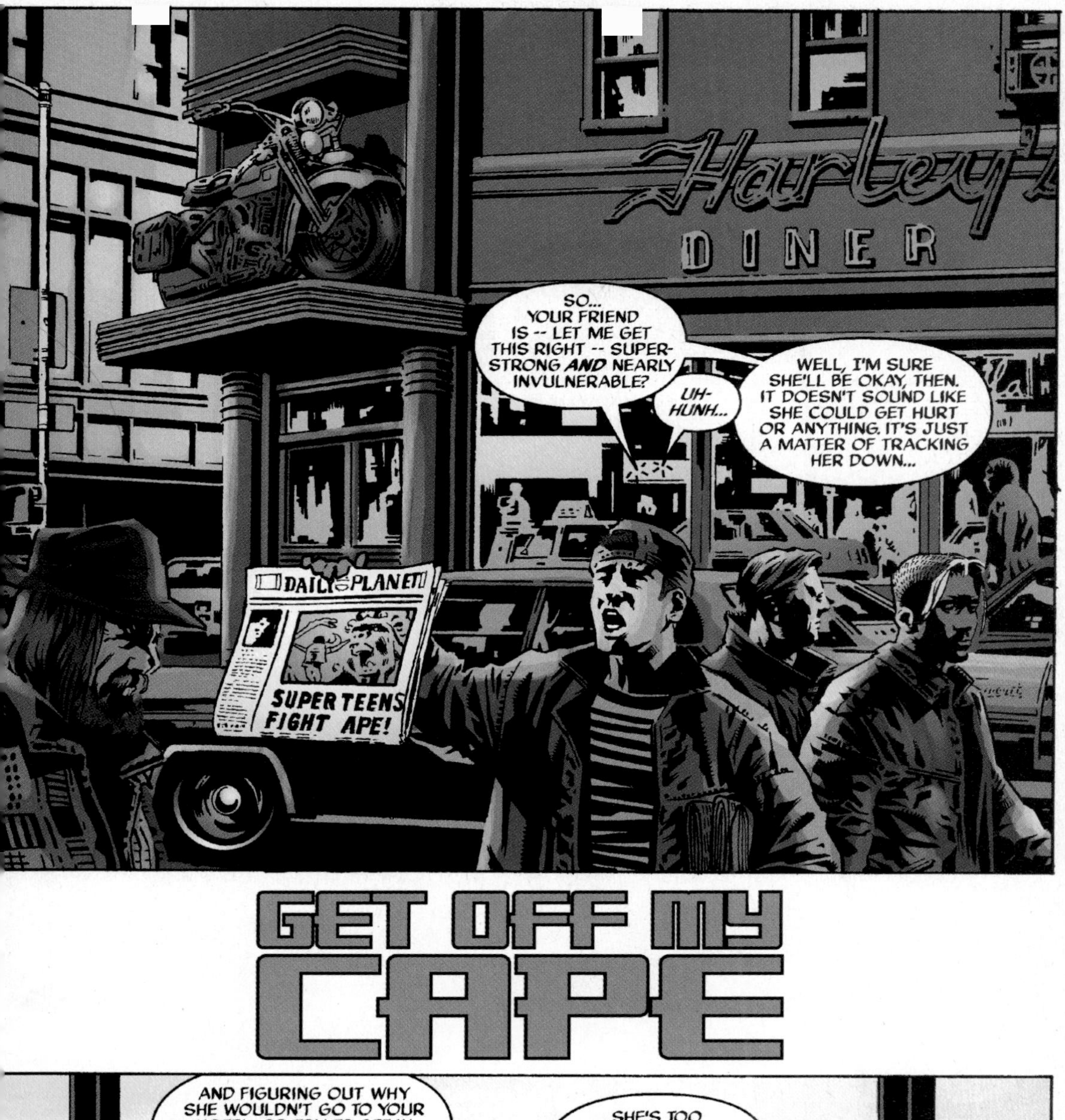
Harley's
DINER
DAILY PLANET
SUPER TEENS FIGHT APE!
SO... YOUR FRIEND IS -- LET ME GET THIS RIGHT -- SUPER-STRONG *AND* NEARLY INVULNERABLE?
UH-HUNH...
WELL, I'M SURE SHE'LL BE OKAY, THEN. IT DOESN'T SOUND LIKE SHE COULD GET HURT OR ANYTHING. IT'S JUST A MATTER OF TRACKING HER DOWN...

GET OFF MY CAPE

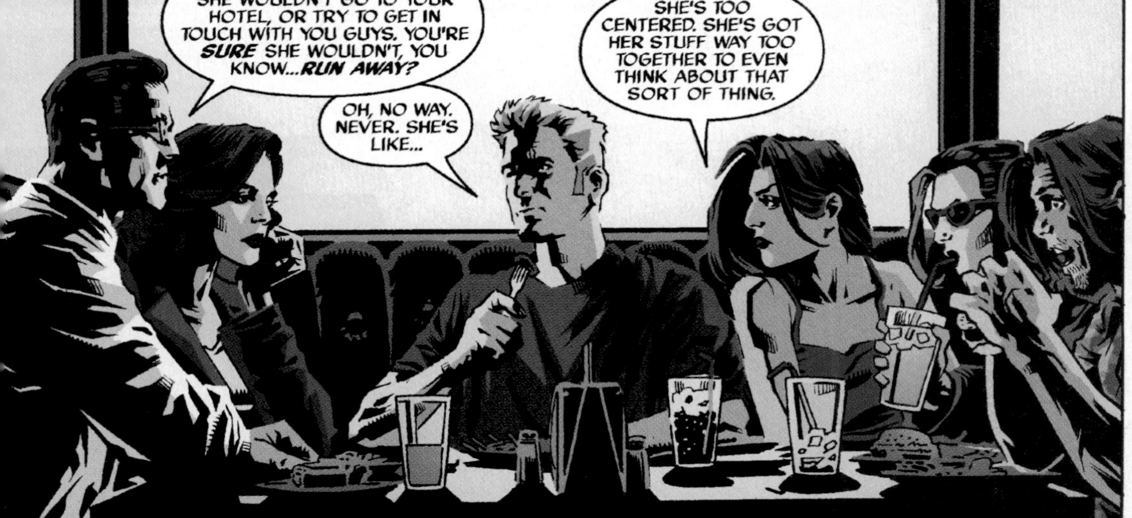
AND FIGURING OUT WHY SHE WOULDN'T GO TO YOUR HOTEL, OR TRY TO GET IN TOUCH WITH YOU GUYS. YOU'RE *SURE* SHE WOULDN'T, YOU KNOW...*RUN AWAY?*
OH, NO WAY. NEVER. SHE'S LIKE...
SHE'S TOO CENTERED. SHE'S GOT HER STUFF WAY TOO TOGETHER TO EVEN THINK ABOUT THAT SORT OF THING.

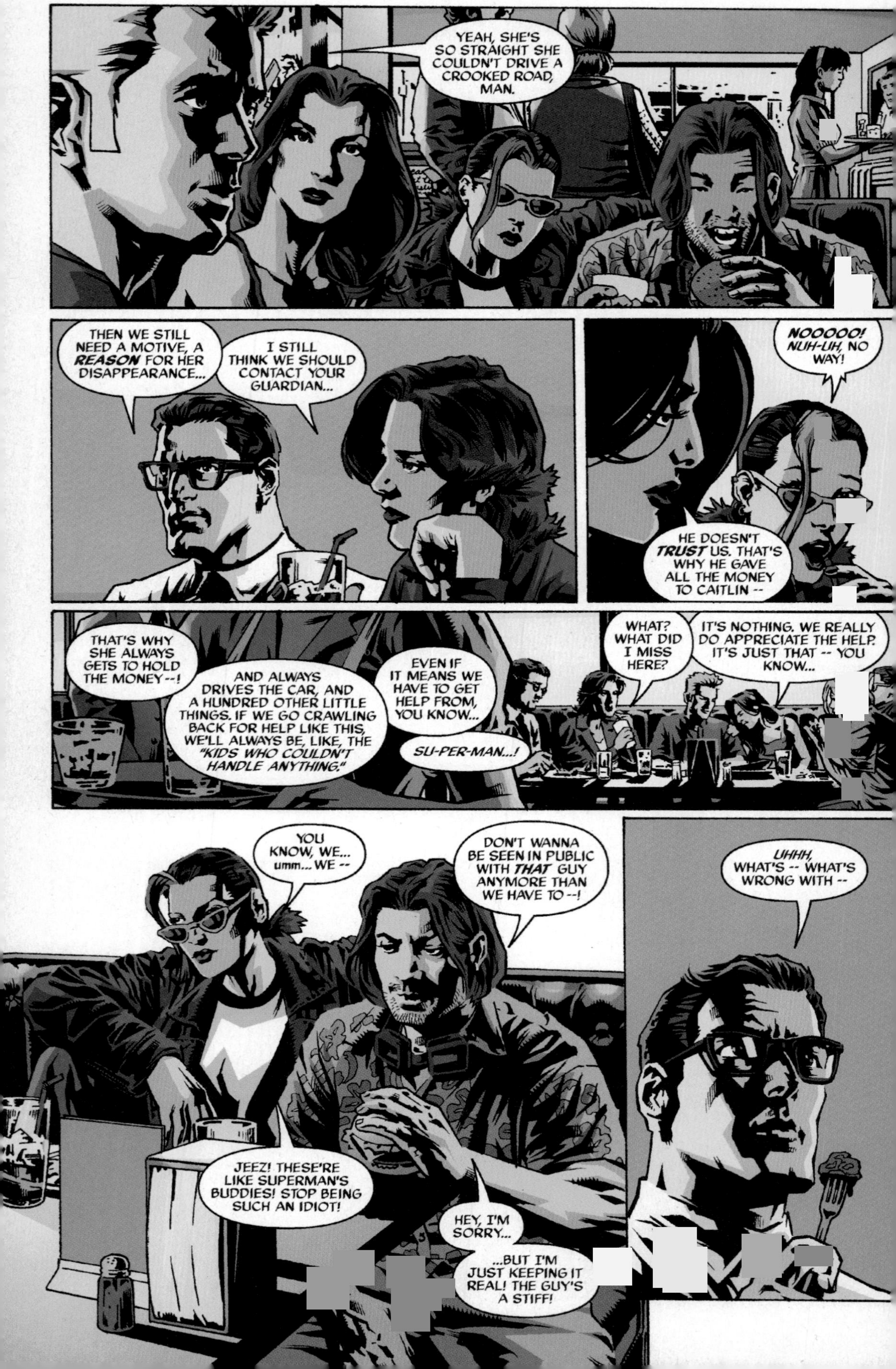
YEAH, SHE'S SO STRAIGHT SHE COULDN'T DRIVE A CROOKED ROAD, MAN.
THEN WE STILL NEED A MOTIVE, A REASON FOR HER DISAPPEARANCE...
I STILL THINK WE SHOULD CONTACT YOUR GUARDIAN...
NOOOOO! NUH-UH, NO WAY!
HE DOESN'T TRUST US. THAT'S WHY HE GAVE ALL THE MONEY TO CAITLIN --
THAT'S WHY SHE ALWAYS GETS TO HOLD THE MONEY--!
AND ALWAYS DRIVES THE CAR, AND A HUNDRED OTHER LITTLE THINGS. IF WE GO CRAWLING BACK FOR HELP LIKE THIS, WE'LL ALWAYS BE, LIKE, THE "KIDS WHO COULDN'T HANDLE ANYTHING."
EVEN IF IT MEANS WE HAVE TO GET HELP FROM, YOU KNOW...
SU-PER-MAN...!
WHAT? WHAT DID I MISS HERE?
IT'S NOTHING. WE REALLY DO APPRECIATE THE HELP. IT'S JUST THAT -- YOU KNOW...
YOU KNOW, WE... umm... WE --
DON'T WANNA BE SEEN IN PUBLIC WITH THAT GUY ANYMORE THAN WE HAVE TO --!
UHHH, WHAT'S -- WHAT'S WRONG WITH --
JEEZ! THESE'RE LIKE SUPERMAN'S BUDDIES! STOP BEING SUCH AN IDIOT!
HEY, I'M SORRY...
...BUT I'M JUST KEEPING IT REAL! THE GUY'S A STIFF!

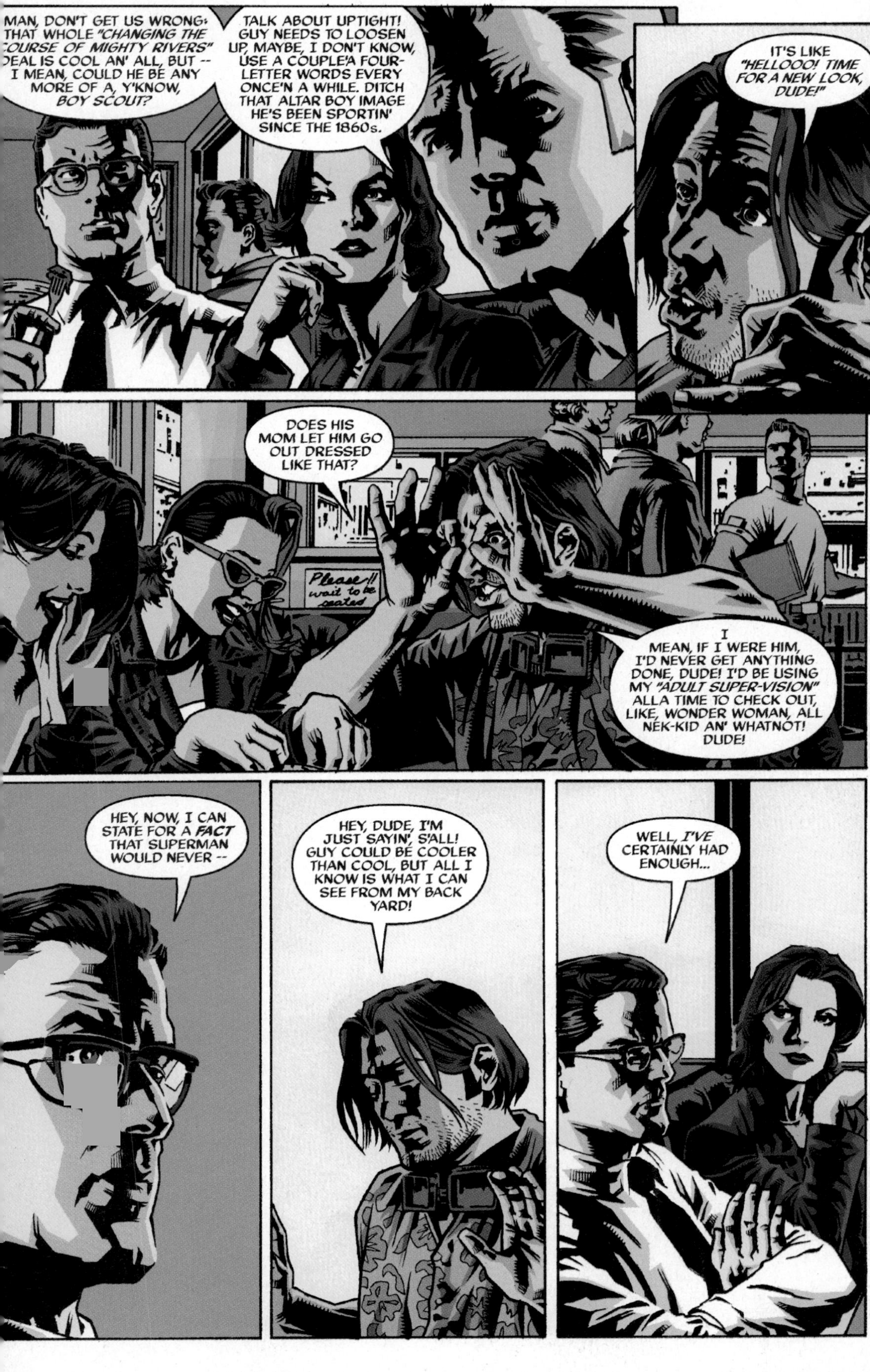
MAN, DON'T GET US WRONG: THAT WHOLE "CHANGING THE COURSE OF MIGHTY RIVERS" DEAL IS COOL AN' ALL, BUT -- I MEAN, COULD HE BE ANY MORE OF A, Y'KNOW, BOY SCOUT?
TALK ABOUT UPTIGHT! GUY NEEDS TO LOOSEN UP, MAYBE, I DON'T KNOW, USE A COUPLE'A FOUR-LETTER WORDS EVERY ONCE'N A WHILE. DITCH THAT ALTAR BOY IMAGE HE'S BEEN SPORTIN' SINCE THE 1860s.
IT'S LIKE "HELLOOO! TIME FOR A NEW LOOK, DUDE!"
DOES HIS MOM LET HIM GO OUT DRESSED LIKE THAT?
Please!! wait to be seated
I MEAN, IF I WERE HIM, I'D NEVER GET ANYTHING DONE, DUDE! I'D BE USING MY "ADULT SUPER-VISION" ALLA TIME TO CHECK OUT, LIKE, WONDER WOMAN, ALL NEK-KID AN' WHATNOT! DUDE!
HEY, NOW, I CAN STATE FOR A FACT THAT SUPERMAN WOULD NEVER --
HEY, DUDE, I'M JUST SAYIN', S'ALL! GUY COULD BE COOLER THAN COOL, BUT ALL I KNOW IS WHAT I CAN SEE FROM MY BACK YARD!
WELL, I'VE CERTAINLY HAD ENOUGH...

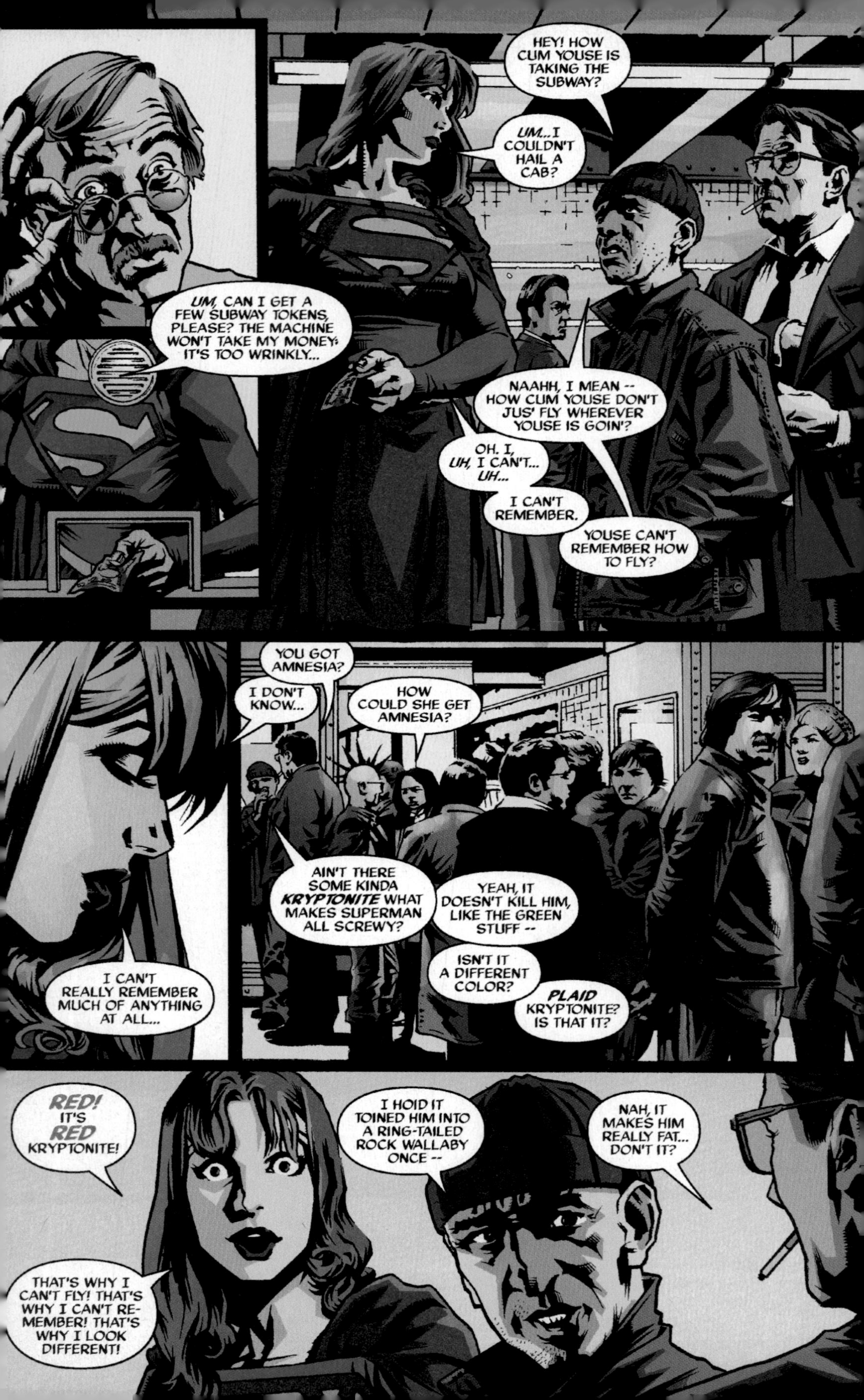
UM, CAN I GET A FEW SUBWAY TOKENS, PLEASE? THE MACHINE WON'T TAKE MY MONEY: IT'S TOO WRINKLY...
HEY! HOW CUM YOUSE IS TAKING THE SUBWAY?
UM... I COULDN'T HAIL A CAB?
NAAHH, I MEAN -- HOW CUM YOUSE DON'T JUS' FLY WHEREVER YOUSE IS GOIN'?
OH. I, UH, I CAN'T... UH...
I CAN'T REMEMBER.
YOUSE CAN'T REMEMBER HOW TO FLY?
I CAN'T REALLY REMEMBER MUCH OF ANYTHING AT ALL...
YOU GOT AMNESIA?
I DON'T KNOW...
HOW COULD SHE GET AMNESIA?
AIN'T THERE SOME KINDA KRYPTONITE WHAT MAKES SUPERMAN ALL SCREWY?
YEAH, IT DOESN'T KILL HIM, LIKE THE GREEN STUFF --
ISN'T IT A DIFFERENT COLOR?
PLAID KRYPTONITE? IS THAT IT?
RED! IT'S RED KRYPTONITE!
I HOID IT TOINED HIM INTO A RING-TAILED ROCK WALLABY ONCE --
NAH, IT MAKES HIM REALLY FAT... DON'T IT?
THAT'S WHY I CAN'T FLY! THAT'S WHY I CAN'T RE-MEMBER! THAT'S WHY I LOOK DIFFERENT!

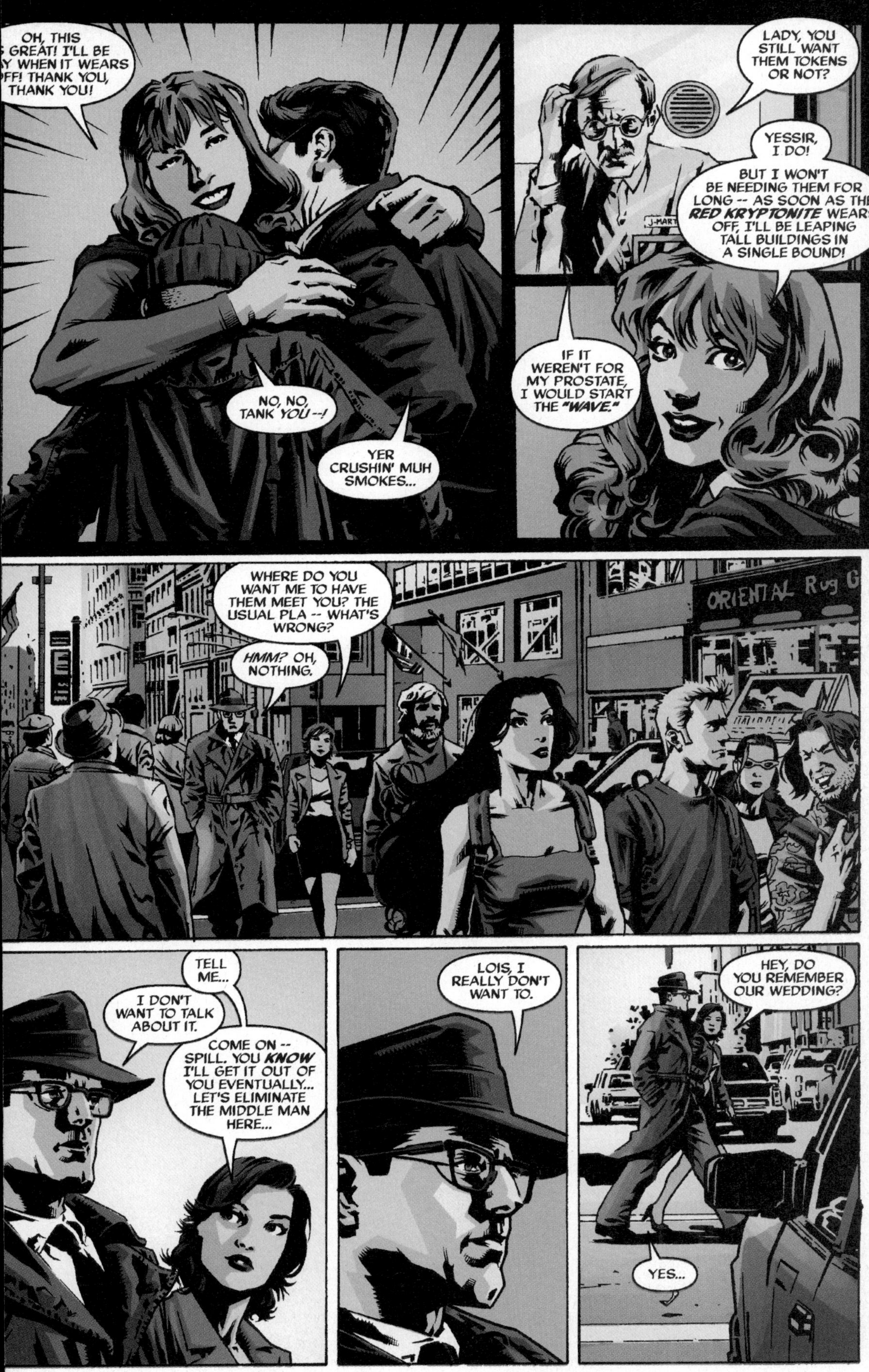

OH, THIS ...S GREAT! I'LL BE ...Y WHEN IT WEARS ...FF! THANK YOU, THANK YOU!
NO, NO, TANK YOU--!
YER CRUSHIN' MUH SMOKES...
LADY, YOU STILL WANT THEM TOKENS OR NOT?
YESSIR, I DO!
BUT I WON'T BE NEEDING THEM FOR LONG -- AS SOON AS THE RED KRYPTONITE WEARS OFF, I'LL BE LEAPING TALL BUILDINGS IN A SINGLE BOUND!
IF IT WEREN'T FOR MY PROSTATE, I WOULD START THE "WAVE."
WHERE DO YOU WANT ME TO HAVE THEM MEET YOU? THE USUAL PLA -- WHAT'S WRONG?
HMM? OH, NOTHING.
ORIENTAL Rug
TELL ME...
I DON'T WANT TO TALK ABOUT IT.
COME ON -- SPILL. YOU KNOW I'LL GET IT OUT OF YOU EVENTUALLY... LET'S ELIMINATE THE MIDDLE MAN HERE...
LOIS, I REALLY DON'T WANT TO.
HEY, DO YOU REMEMBER OUR WEDDING?
YES...

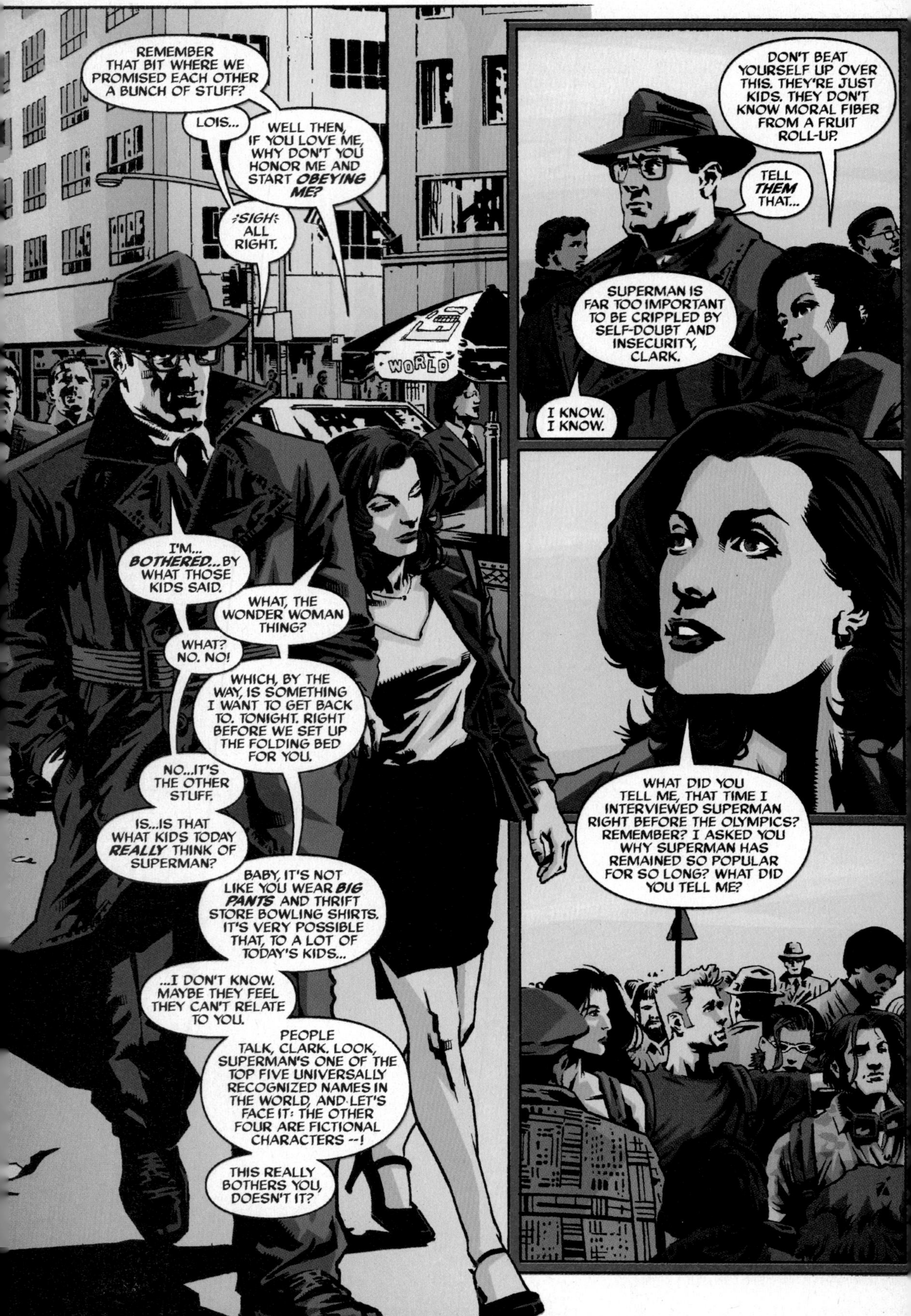
REMEMBER THAT BIT WHERE WE PROMISED EACH OTHER A BUNCH OF STUFF?
LOIS...
WELL THEN, IF YOU LOVE ME, WHY DON'T YOU HONOR ME AND START *OBEYING ME?*
:SIGH: ALL RIGHT.
WORLD
I'M... *BOTHERED*... BY WHAT THOSE KIDS SAID.
WHAT, THE WONDER WOMAN THING?
WHAT? NO. NO!
WHICH, BY THE WAY, IS SOMETHING I WANT TO GET BACK TO. TONIGHT. RIGHT BEFORE WE SET UP THE FOLDING BED FOR YOU.
NO...IT'S THE OTHER STUFF.
IS...IS THAT WHAT KIDS TODAY *REALLY* THINK OF SUPERMAN?
BABY, IT'S NOT LIKE YOU WEAR *BIG PANTS* AND THRIFT STORE BOWLING SHIRTS. IT'S VERY POSSIBLE THAT, TO A LOT OF TODAY'S KIDS...
...I DON'T KNOW. MAYBE THEY FEEL THEY CAN'T RELATE TO YOU.
PEOPLE TALK, CLARK. LOOK, SUPERMAN'S ONE OF THE TOP FIVE UNIVERSALLY RECOGNIZED NAMES IN THE WORLD, AND LET'S FACE IT: THE OTHER FOUR ARE FICTIONAL CHARACTERS --!
THIS REALLY BOTHERS YOU, DOESN'T IT?
DON'T BEAT YOURSELF UP OVER THIS. THEY'RE JUST KIDS. THEY DON'T KNOW MORAL FIBER FROM A FRUIT ROLL-UP.
TELL *THEM* THAT...
SUPERMAN IS FAR TOO IMPORTANT TO BE CRIPPLED BY SELF-DOUBT AND INSECURITY, CLARK.
I KNOW. I KNOW.
WHAT DID YOU TELL ME, THAT TIME I INTERVIEWED SUPERMAN RIGHT BEFORE THE OLYMPICS? REMEMBER? I ASKED YOU WHY SUPERMAN HAS REMAINED SO POPULAR FOR SO LONG? WHAT DID YOU TELL ME?

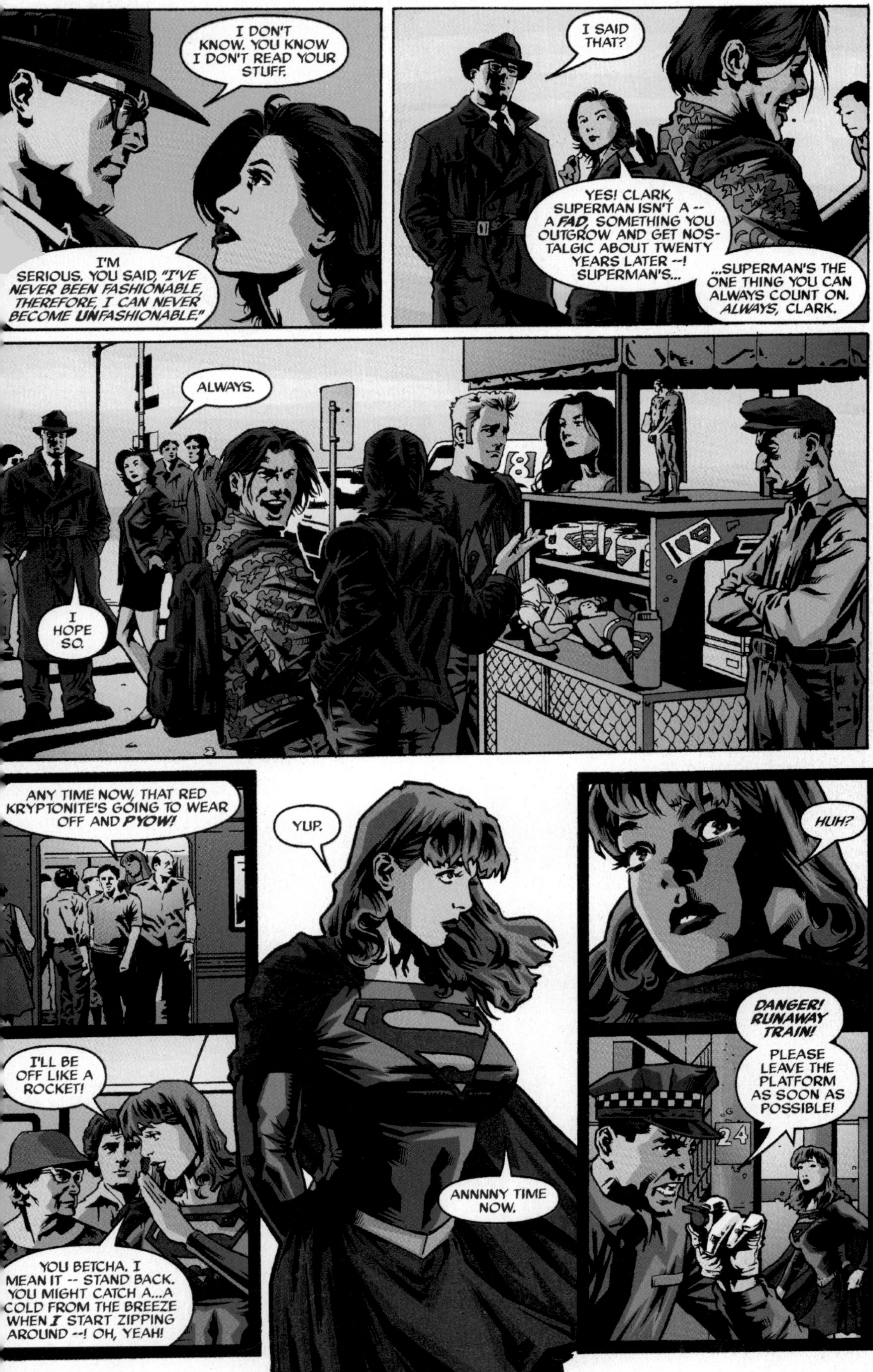
I DON'T KNOW. YOU KNOW I DON'T READ YOUR STUFF.
I'M SERIOUS. YOU SAID, "I'VE NEVER BEEN FASHIONABLE, THEREFORE, I CAN NEVER BECOME UNFASHIONABLE."
I SAID THAT?
YES! CLARK, SUPERMAN ISN'T A -- A FAD, SOMETHING YOU OUTGROW AND GET NOS-TALGIC ABOUT TWENTY YEARS LATER --! SUPERMAN'S...
...SUPERMAN'S THE ONE THING YOU CAN ALWAYS COUNT ON. ALWAYS, CLARK.
ALWAYS.
I HOPE SO.
ANY TIME NOW, THAT RED KRYPTONITE'S GOING TO WEAR OFF AND PYOW!
I'LL BE OFF LIKE A ROCKET!
YOU BETCHA. I MEAN IT -- STAND BACK. YOU MIGHT CATCH A...A COLD FROM THE BREEZE WHEN I START ZIPPING AROUND --! OH, YEAH!
YUP.
ANNNNY TIME NOW.
HUH?
DANGER! RUNAWAY TRAIN!
PLEASE LEAVE THE PLATFORM AS SOON AS POSSIBLE!

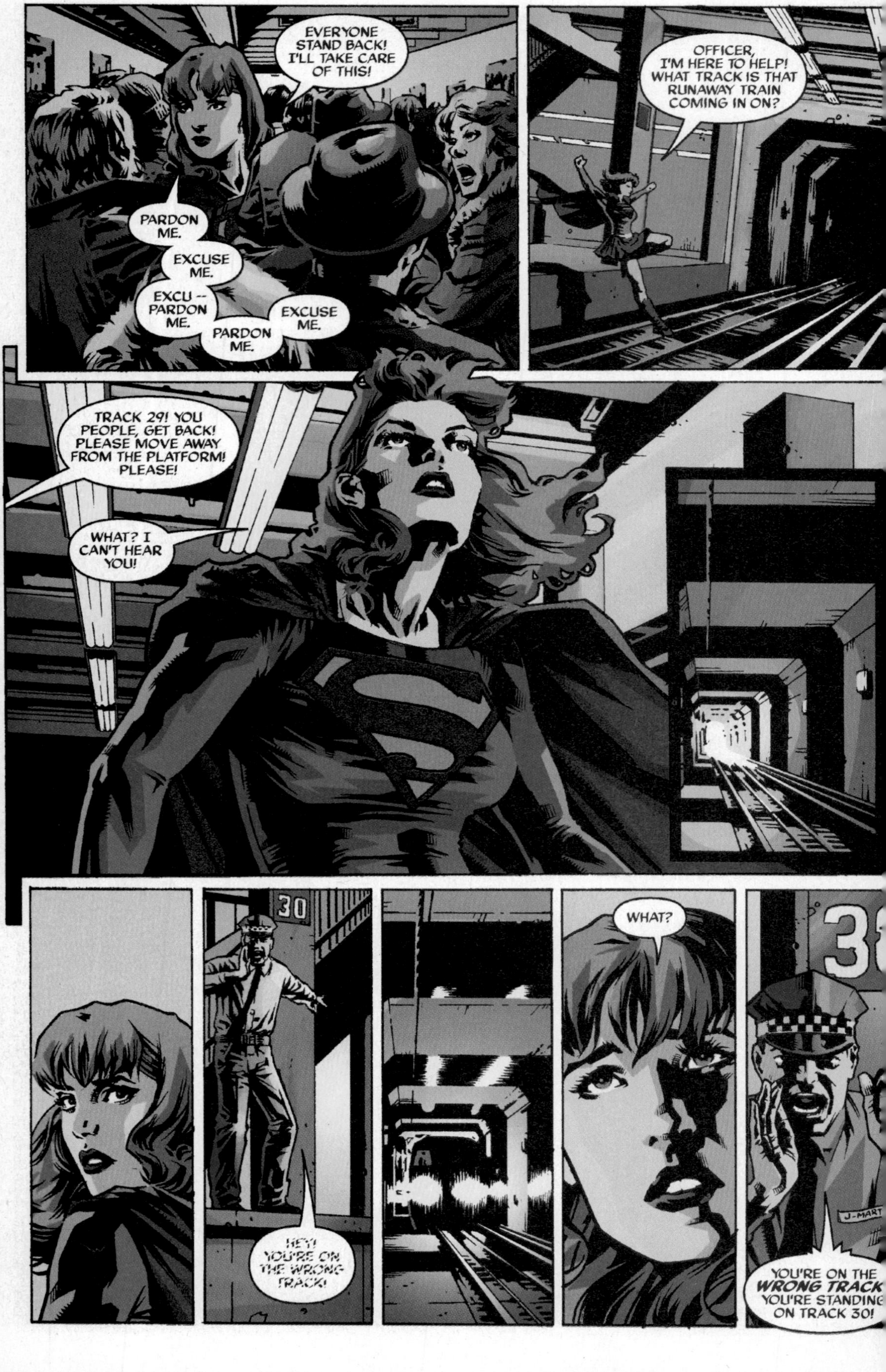
EVERYONE STAND BACK! I'LL TAKE CARE OF THIS!
PARDON ME.
EXCUSE ME.
EXCU -- PARDON ME.
PARDON ME.
EXCUSE ME.
OFFICER, I'M HERE TO HELP! WHAT TRACK IS THAT RUNAWAY TRAIN COMING IN ON?
TRACK 29! YOU PEOPLE, GET BACK! PLEASE MOVE AWAY FROM THE PLATFORM! PLEASE!
WHAT? I CAN'T HEAR YOU!
30
HEY! YOU'RE ON THE WRONG TRACK!
WHAT?
YOU'RE ON THE WRONG TRACK YOU'RE STANDING ON TRACK 30!

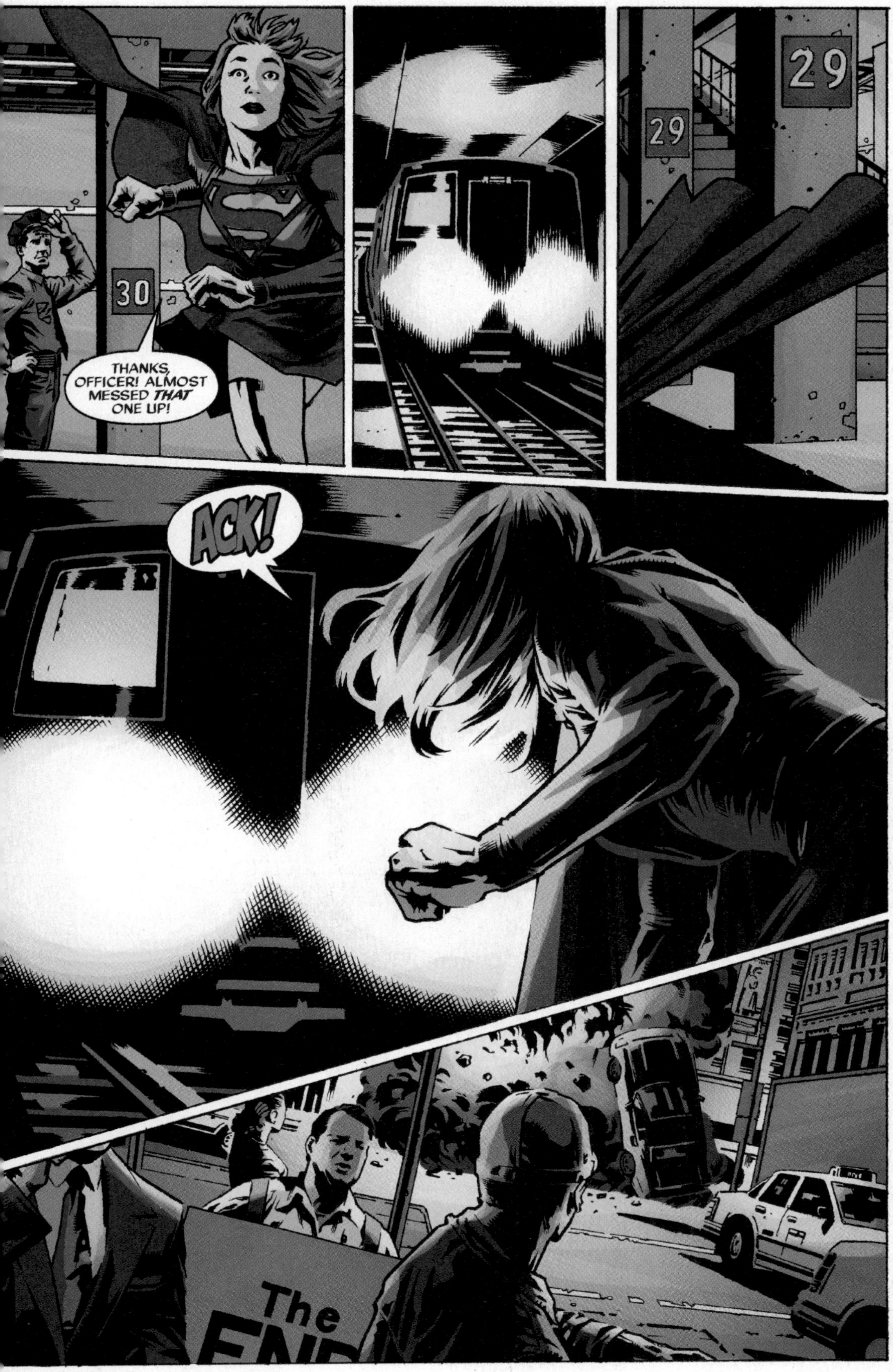
30
THANKS, OFFICER! ALMOST MESSED *THAT* ONE UP!
29
29
ACK!
The END

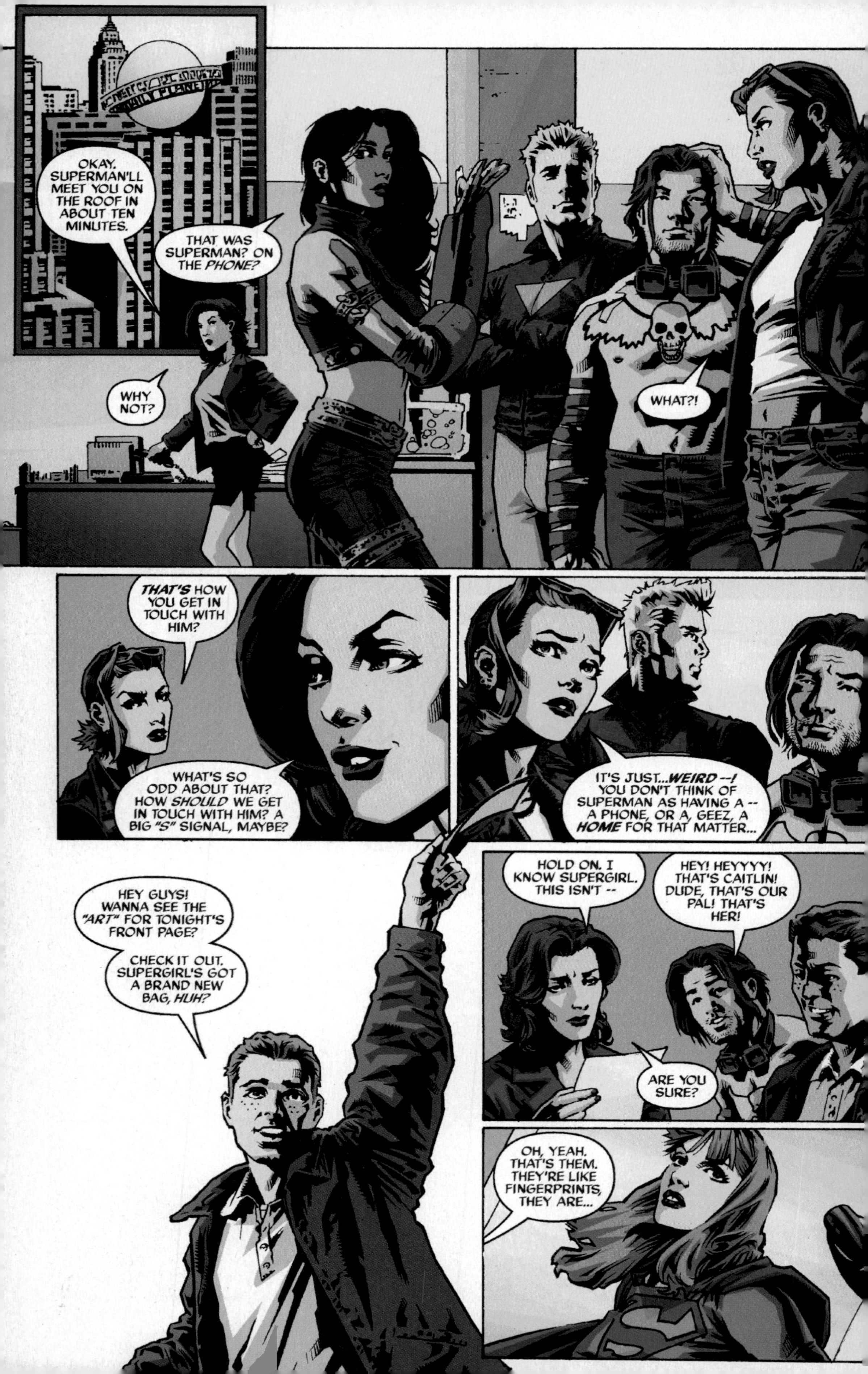
OKAY. SUPERMAN'LL MEET YOU ON THE ROOF IN ABOUT TEN MINUTES.
THAT WAS SUPERMAN? ON THE PHONE?
WHY NOT?
WHAT?!
THAT'S HOW YOU GET IN TOUCH WITH HIM?
WHAT'S SO ODD ABOUT THAT? HOW SHOULD WE GET IN TOUCH WITH HIM? A BIG "S" SIGNAL, MAYBE?
IT'S JUST...WEIRD --! YOU DON'T THINK OF SUPERMAN AS HAVING A -- A PHONE, OR A, GEEZ, A HOME FOR THAT MATTER...
HEY GUYS! WANNA SEE THE "ART" FOR TONIGHT'S FRONT PAGE?
CHECK IT OUT. SUPERGIRL'S GOT A BRAND NEW BAG, HUH?
HOLD ON. I KNOW SUPERGIRL. THIS ISN'T --
HEY! HEYYYY! THAT'S CAITLIN! DUDE, THAT'S OUR PAL! THAT'S HER!
ARE YOU SURE?
OH, YEAH. THAT'S THEM. THEY'RE LIKE FINGERPRINTS, THEY ARE...

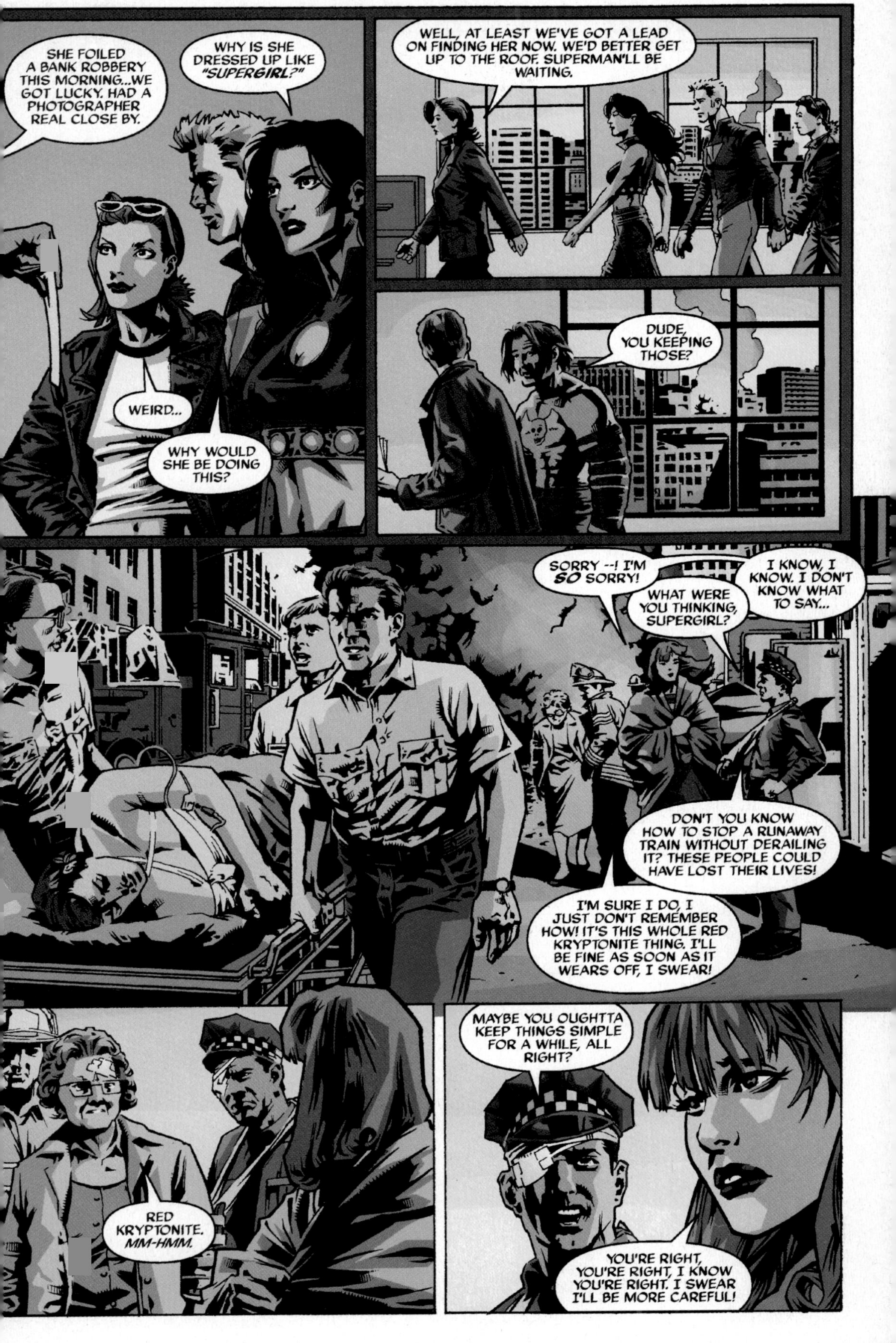
SHE FOILED A BANK ROBBERY THIS MORNING...WE GOT LUCKY. HAD A PHOTOGRAPHER REAL CLOSE BY.
WHY IS SHE DRESSED UP LIKE "SUPERGIRL?"
WEIRD...
WHY WOULD SHE BE DOING THIS?
WELL, AT LEAST WE'VE GOT A LEAD ON FINDING HER NOW. WE'D BETTER GET UP TO THE ROOF. SUPERMAN'LL BE WAITING.
DUDE, YOU KEEPING THOSE?
SORRY --! I'M SO SORRY!
WHAT WERE YOU THINKING, SUPERGIRL?
I KNOW, I KNOW. I DON'T KNOW WHAT TO SAY...
DON'T YOU KNOW HOW TO STOP A RUNAWAY TRAIN WITHOUT DERAILING IT? THESE PEOPLE COULD HAVE LOST THEIR LIVES!
I'M SURE I DO, I JUST DON'T REMEMBER HOW! IT'S THIS WHOLE RED KRYPTONITE THING. I'LL BE FINE AS SOON AS IT WEARS OFF, I SWEAR!
RED KRYPTONITE. MM-HMM.
MAYBE YOU OUGHTTA KEEP THINGS SIMPLE FOR A WHILE, ALL RIGHT?
YOU'RE RIGHT, YOU'RE RIGHT, I KNOW YOU'RE RIGHT. I SWEAR I'LL BE MORE CAREFUL!

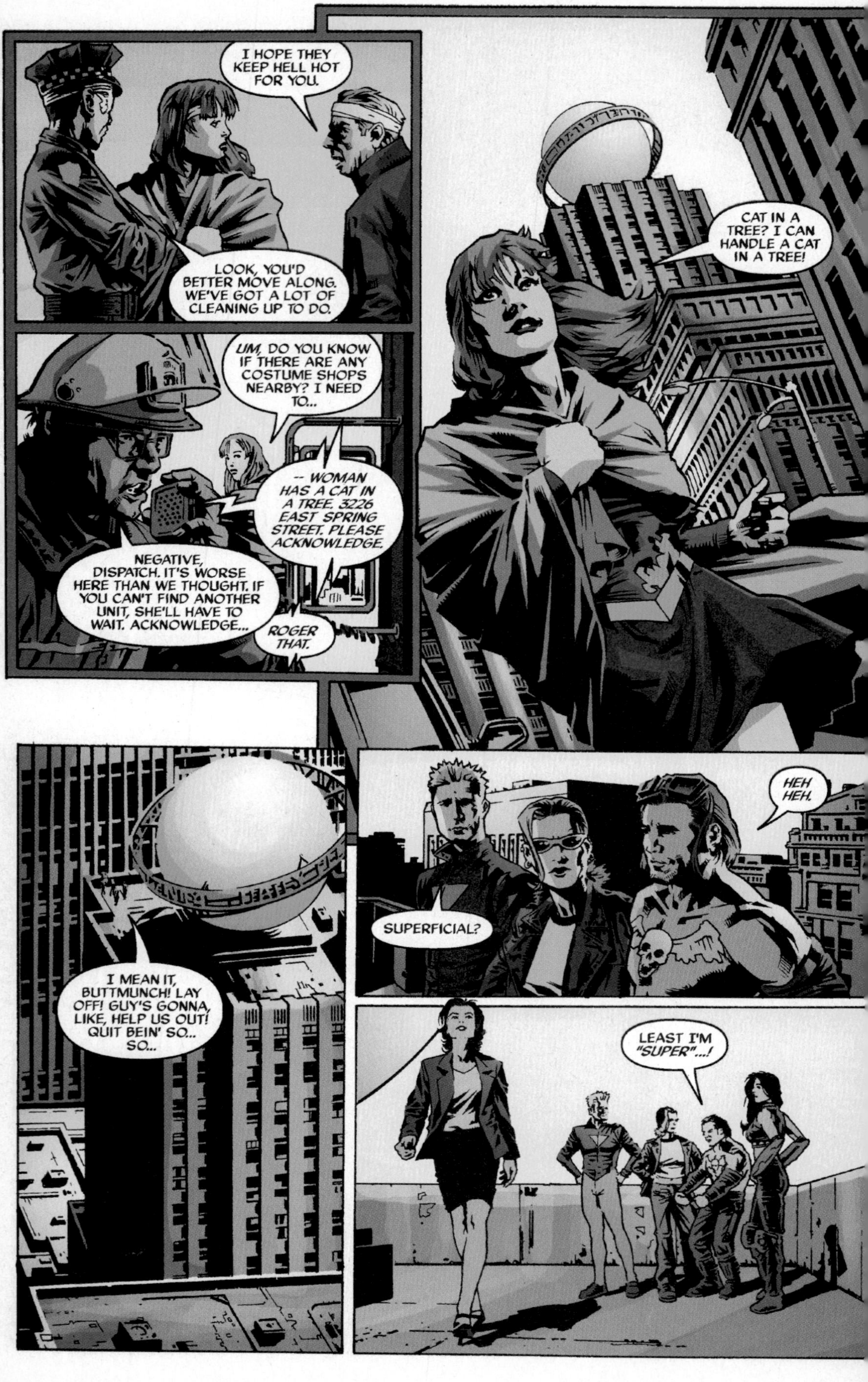
I HOPE THEY KEEP HELL HOT FOR YOU.
LOOK, YOU'D BETTER MOVE ALONG. WE'VE GOT A LOT OF CLEANING UP TO DO.
CAT IN A TREE? I CAN HANDLE A CAT IN A TREE!
UM, DO YOU KNOW IF THERE ARE ANY COSTUME SHOPS NEARBY? I NEED TO...
-- WOMAN HAS A CAT IN A TREE. 3226 EAST SPRING STREET. PLEASE ACKNOWLEDGE.
NEGATIVE, DISPATCH. IT'S WORSE HERE THAN WE THOUGHT. IF YOU CAN'T FIND ANOTHER UNIT, SHE'LL HAVE TO WAIT. ACKNOWLEDGE...
ROGER THAT.
I MEAN IT, BUTTMUNCH! LAY OFF! GUY'S GONNA, LIKE, HELP US OUT! QUIT BEIN' SO... SO...
SUPERFICIAL?
HEH HEH.
LEAST I'M "SUPER"...!

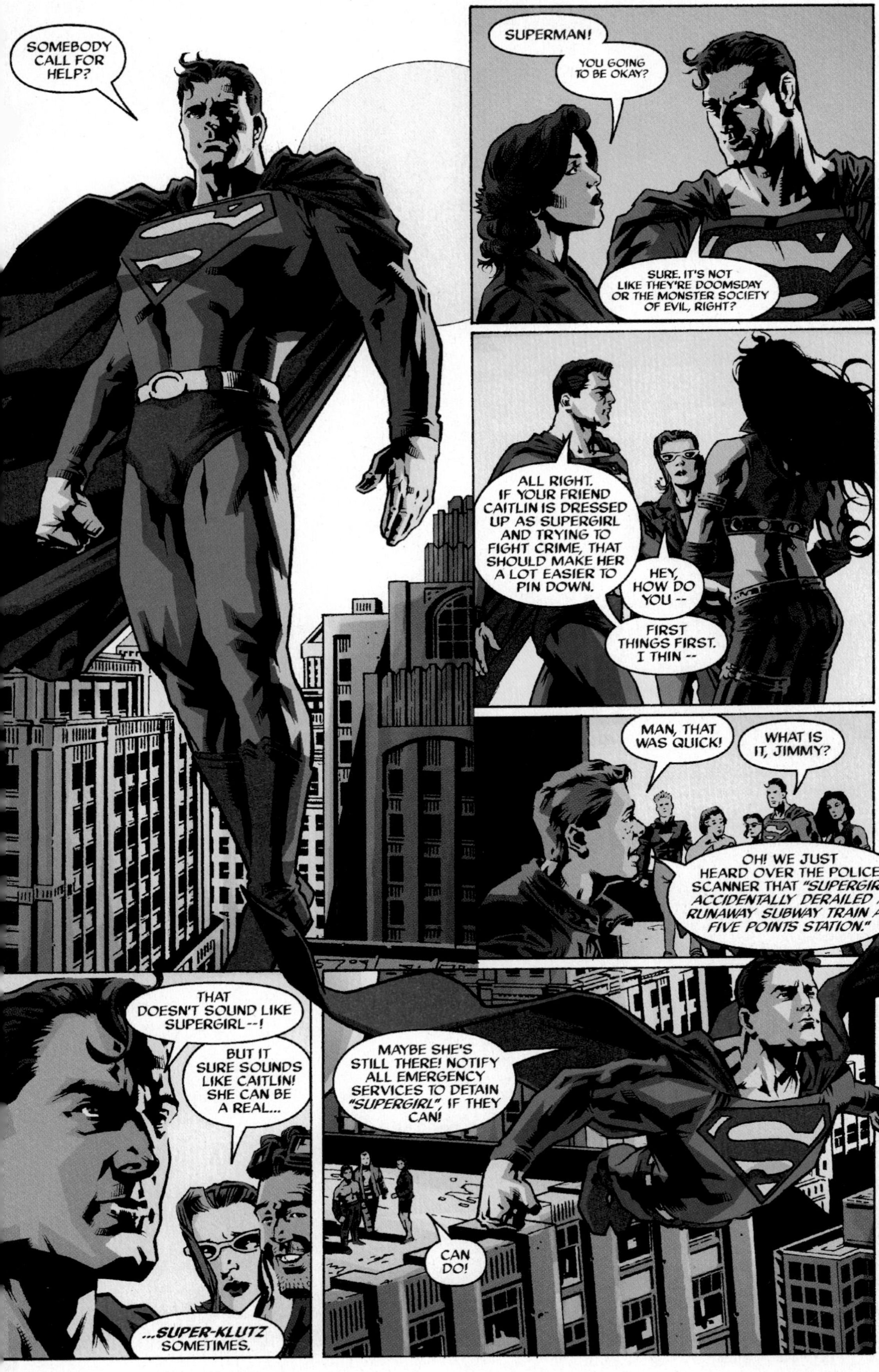
SOMEBODY CALL FOR HELP?
SUPERMAN!
YOU GOING TO BE OKAY?
SURE. IT'S NOT LIKE THEY'RE DOOMSDAY OR THE MONSTER SOCIETY OF EVIL, RIGHT?
ALL RIGHT. IF YOUR FRIEND CAITLIN IS DRESSED UP AS SUPERGIRL AND TRYING TO FIGHT CRIME, THAT SHOULD MAKE HER A LOT EASIER TO PIN DOWN.
HEY, HOW DO YOU --
FIRST THINGS FIRST. I THIN --
MAN, THAT WAS QUICK!
WHAT IS IT, JIMMY?
OH! WE JUST HEARD OVER THE POLICE SCANNER THAT "SUPERGIRL ACCIDENTALLY DERAILED A RUNAWAY SUBWAY TRAIN AT FIVE POINTS STATION."
THAT DOESN'T SOUND LIKE SUPERGIRL--!
BUT IT SURE SOUNDS LIKE CAITLIN! SHE CAN BE A REAL...
...SUPER-KLUTZ SOMETIMES.
MAYBE SHE'S STILL THERE! NOTIFY ALL EMERGENCY SERVICES TO DETAIN "SUPERGIRL", IF THEY CAN!
CAN DO!

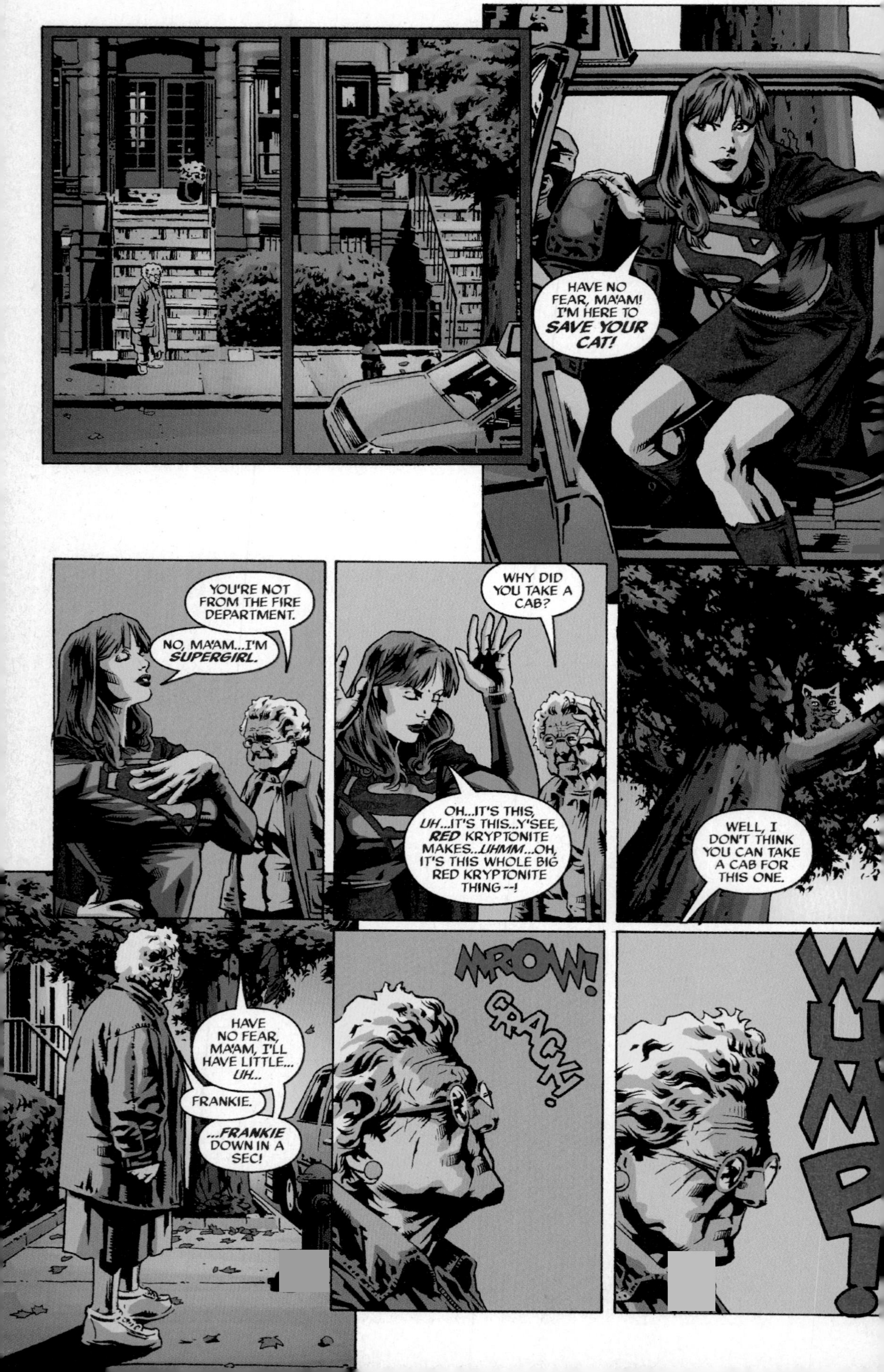
HAVE NO FEAR, MA'AM! I'M HERE TO SAVE YOUR CAT!
YOU'RE NOT FROM THE FIRE DEPARTMENT.
NO, MA'AM...I'M SUPERGIRL.
WHY DID YOU TAKE A CAB?
OH...IT'S THIS, UH...IT'S THIS...Y'SEE, RED KRYPTONITE MAKES...UHMM...OH, IT'S THIS WHOLE BIG RED KRYPTONITE THING--!
WELL, I DON'T THINK YOU CAN TAKE A CAB FOR THIS ONE.
HAVE NO FEAR, MA'AM, I'LL HAVE LITTLE... UH...
FRANKIE.
...FRANKIE DOWN IN A SEC!
MROW!
CRACK!
WUMP!

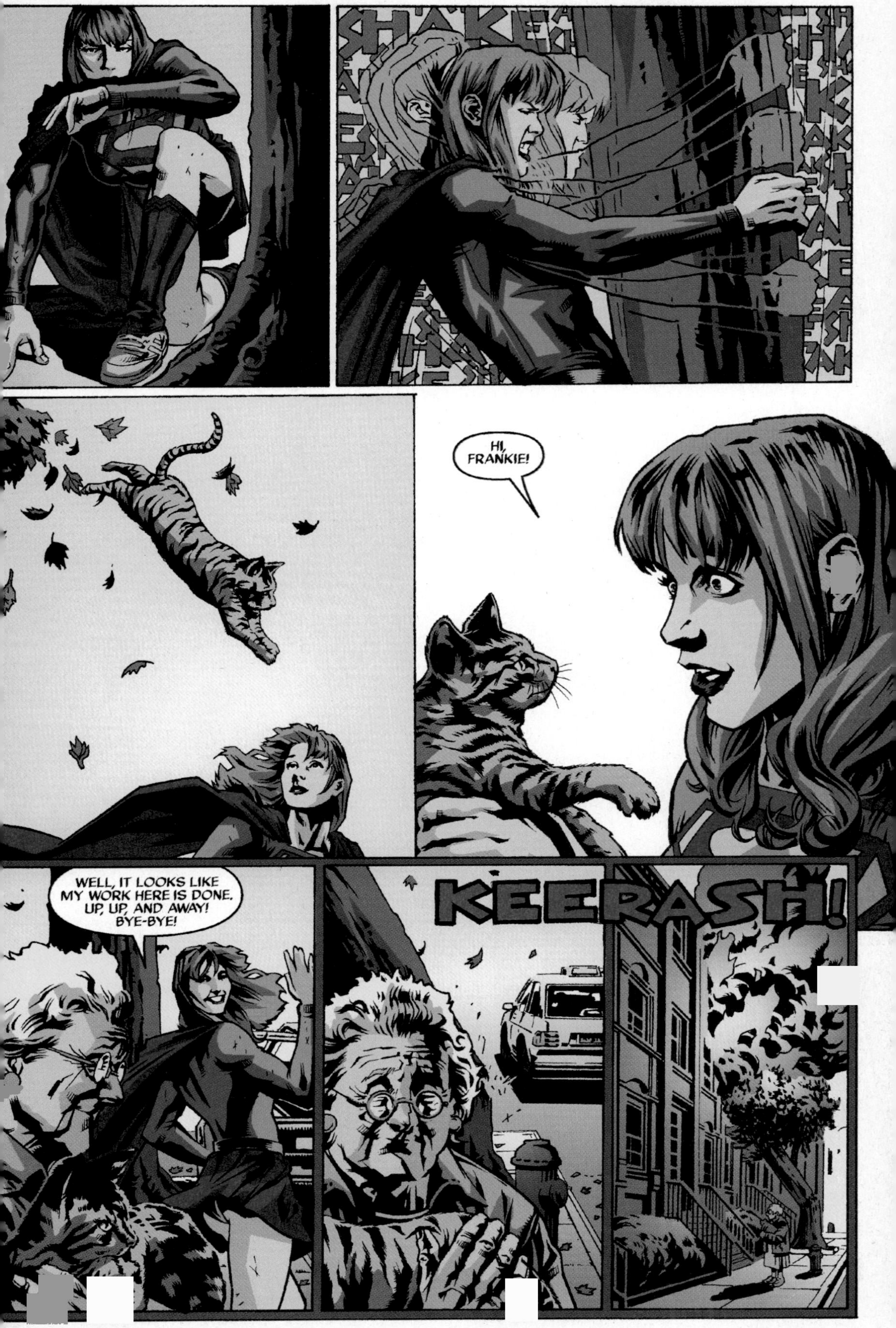
SHAKE
HI, FRANKIE!
WELL, IT LOOKS LIKE MY WORK HERE IS DONE. UP, UP, AND AWAY! BYE-BYE!
KEERASH!

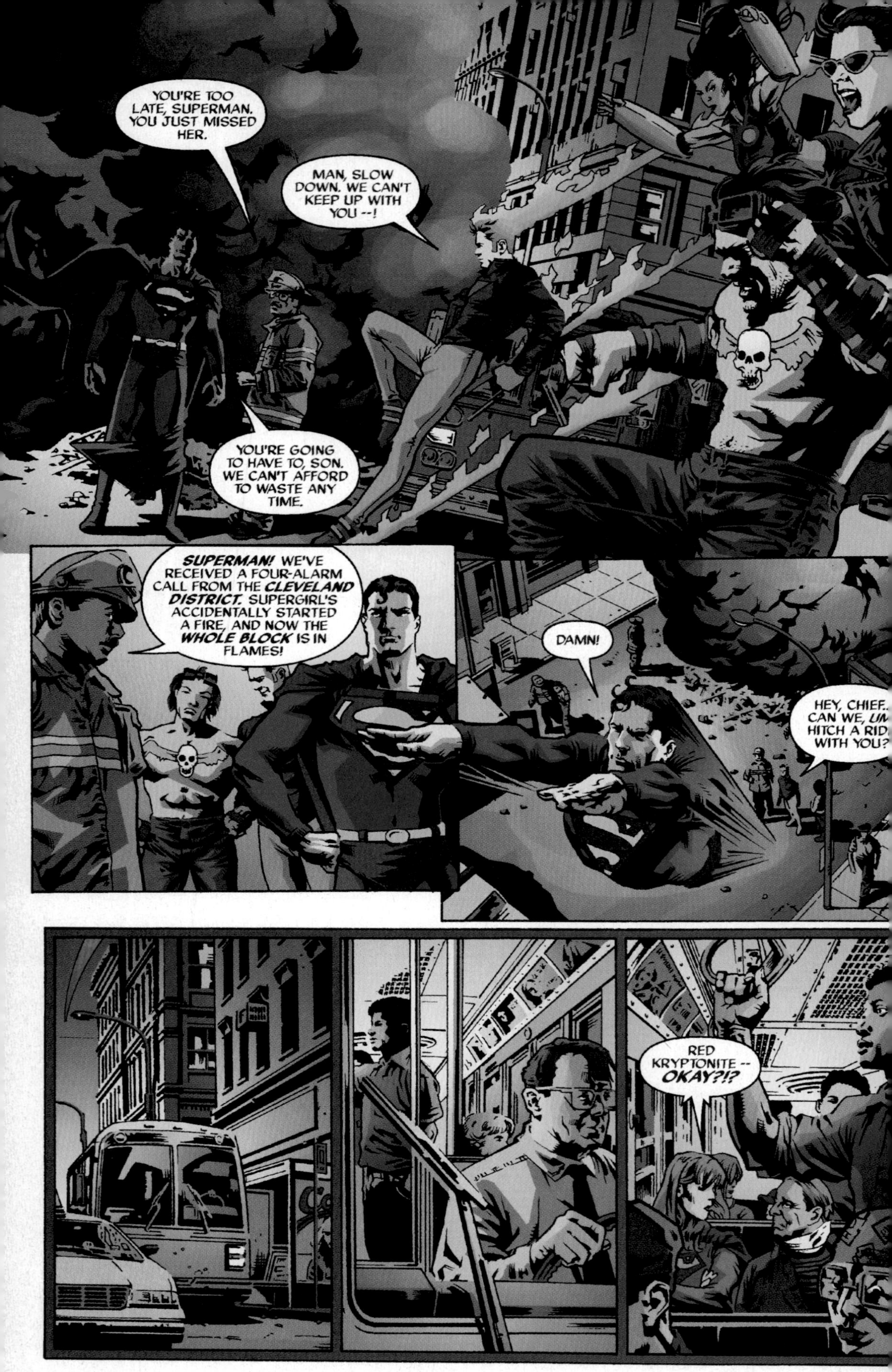

YOU'RE TOO LATE, SUPERMAN. YOU JUST MISSED HER.
MAN, SLOW DOWN. WE CAN'T KEEP UP WITH YOU --!
YOU'RE GOING TO HAVE TO, SON. WE CAN'T AFFORD TO WASTE ANY TIME.
SUPERMAN! WE'VE RECEIVED A FOUR-ALARM CALL FROM THE CLEVELAND DISTRICT. SUPERGIRL'S ACCIDENTALLY STARTED A FIRE, AND NOW THE WHOLE BLOCK IS IN FLAMES!
DAMN!
HEY, CHIEF... CAN WE, UM, HITCH A RIDE WITH YOU?
RED KRYPTONITE -- OKAY?!?

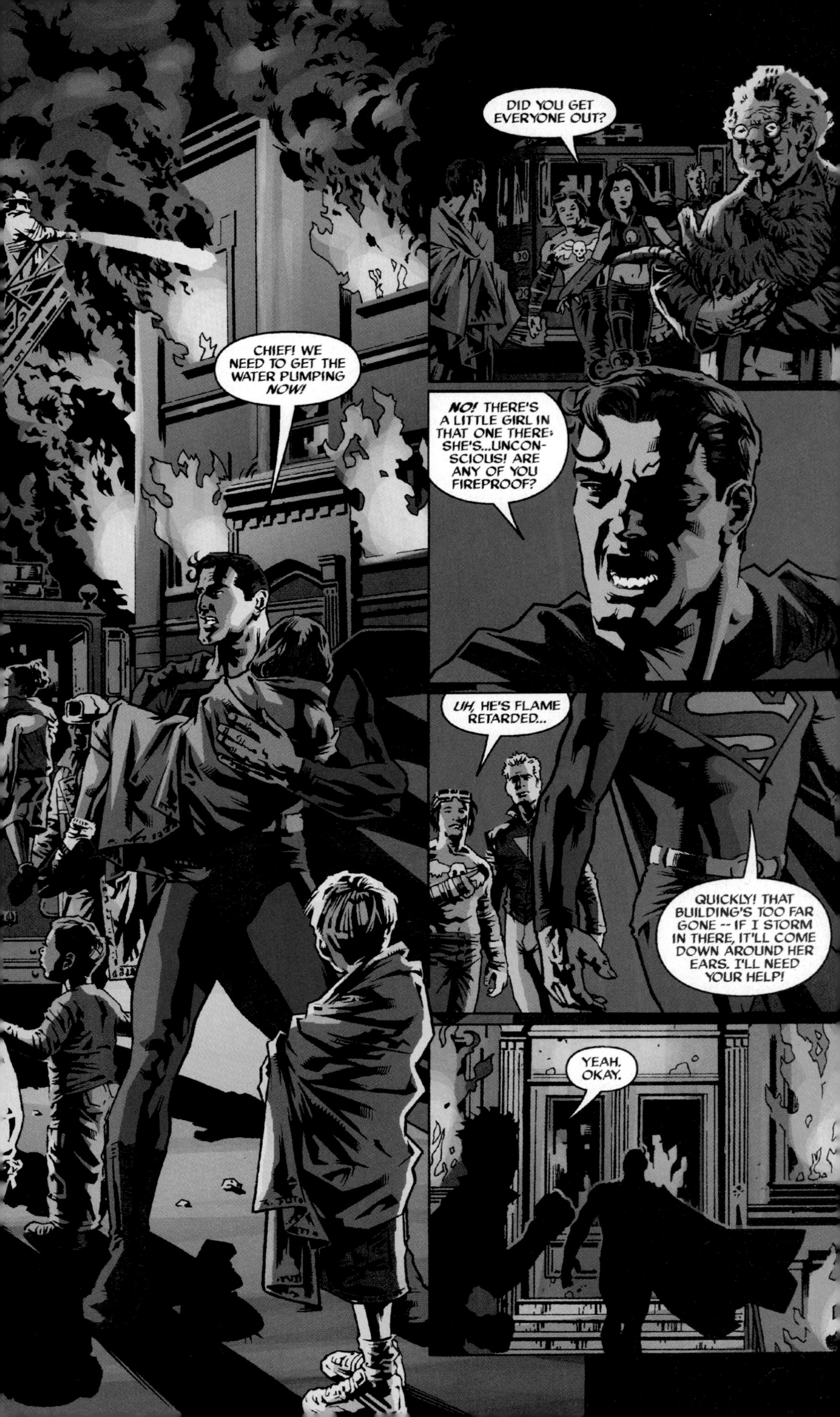
CHIEF! WE NEED TO GET THE WATER PUMPING *NOW!*
DID YOU GET EVERYONE OUT?
NO! THERE'S A LITTLE GIRL IN THAT ONE THERE; SHE'S...UNCONSCIOUS! ARE ANY OF YOU FIREPROOF?
UH, HE'S FLAME RETARDED...
QUICKLY! THAT BUILDING'S TOO FAR GONE -- IF I STORM IN THERE, IT'LL COME DOWN AROUND HER EARS. I'LL NEED YOUR HELP!
YEAH. OKAY.

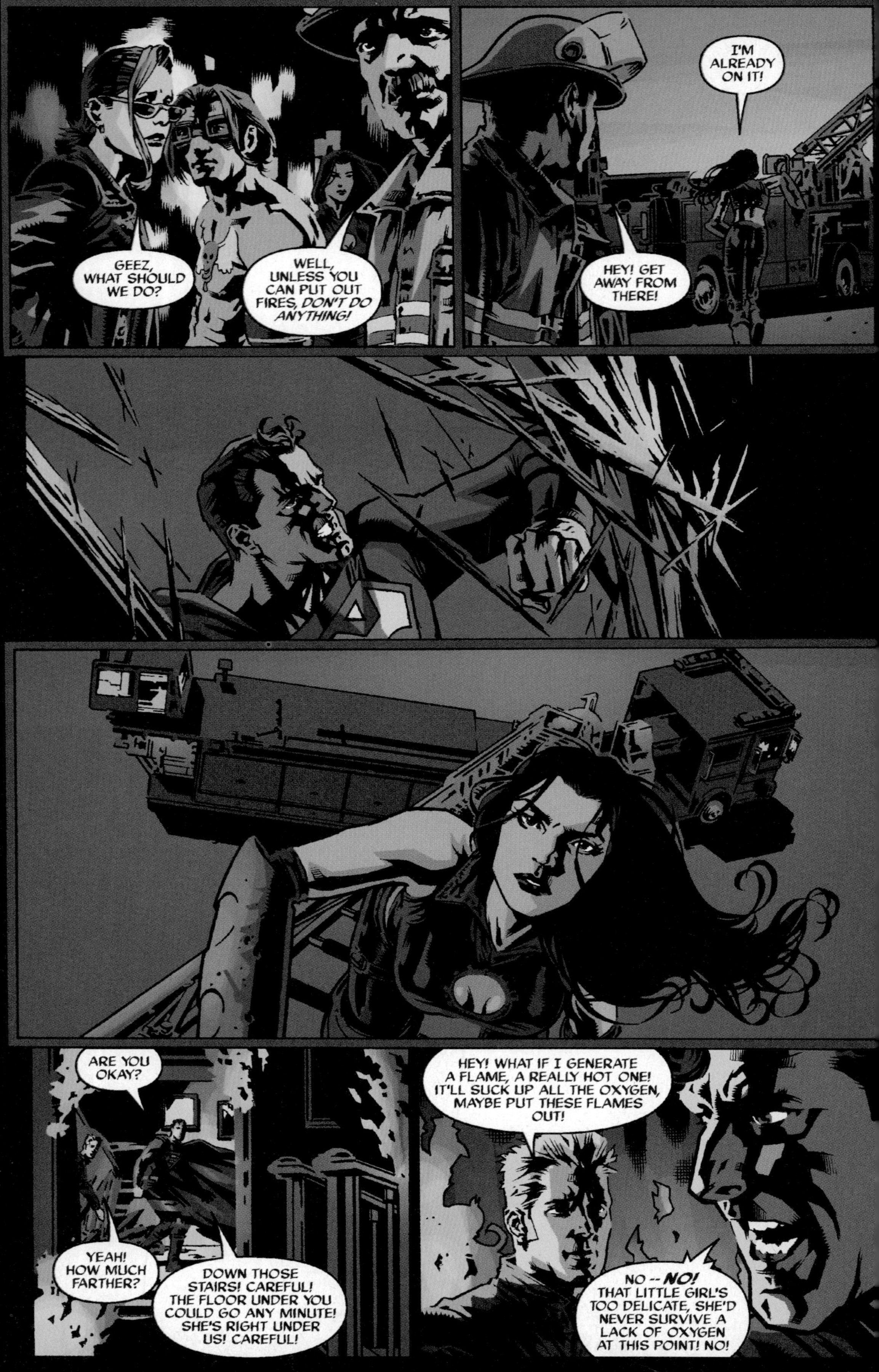
GEEZ, WHAT SHOULD WE DO?
WELL, UNLESS YOU CAN PUT OUT FIRES, *DON'T DO ANYTHING!*
HEY! GET AWAY FROM THERE!
I'M ALREADY ON IT!
ARE YOU OKAY?
YEAH! HOW MUCH FARTHER?
DOWN THOSE STAIRS! CAREFUL! THE FLOOR UNDER YOU COULD GO ANY MINUTE! SHE'S RIGHT UNDER US! CAREFUL!
HEY! WHAT IF I GENERATE A FLAME, A REALLY HOT ONE! IT'LL SUCK UP ALL THE OXYGEN, MAYBE PUT THESE FLAMES OUT!
NO -- ***NO!*** THAT LITTLE GIRL'S TOO DELICATE, SHE'D NEVER SURVIVE A LACK OF OXYGEN AT THIS POINT! NO!

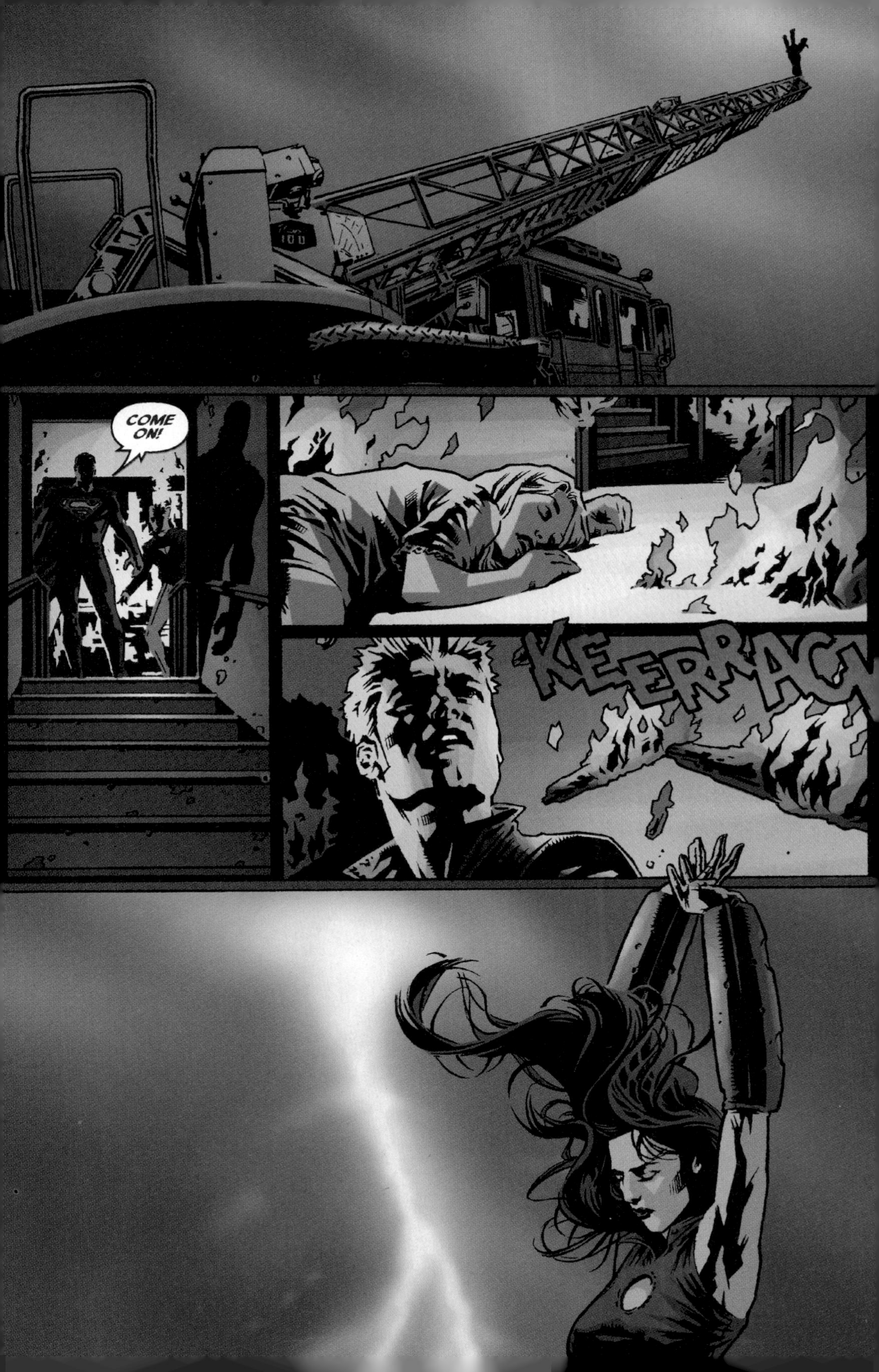
COME ON!
KEERRAC

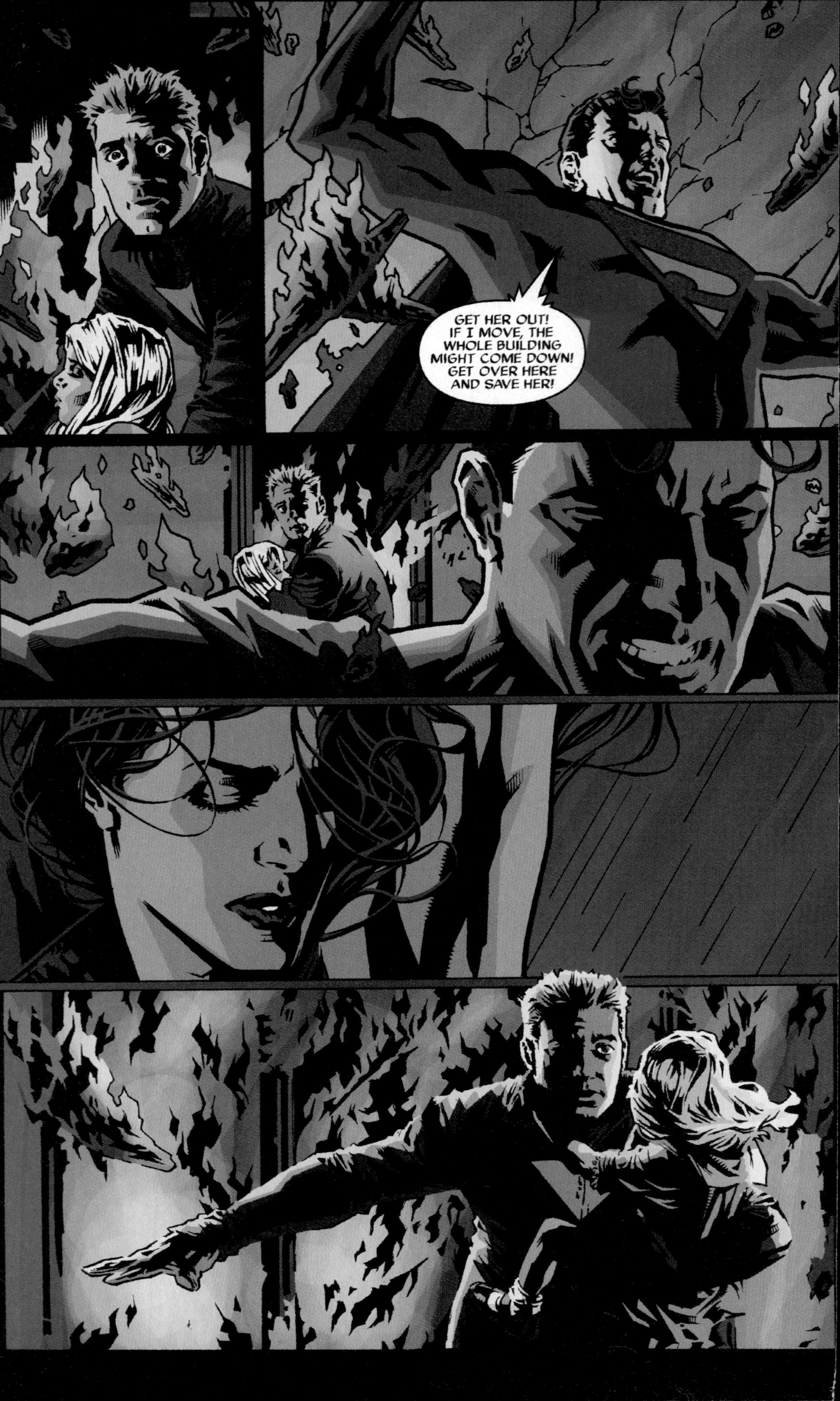
GET HER OUT! IF I MOVE, THE WHOLE BUILDING MIGHT COME DOWN! GET OVER HERE AND SAVE HER!

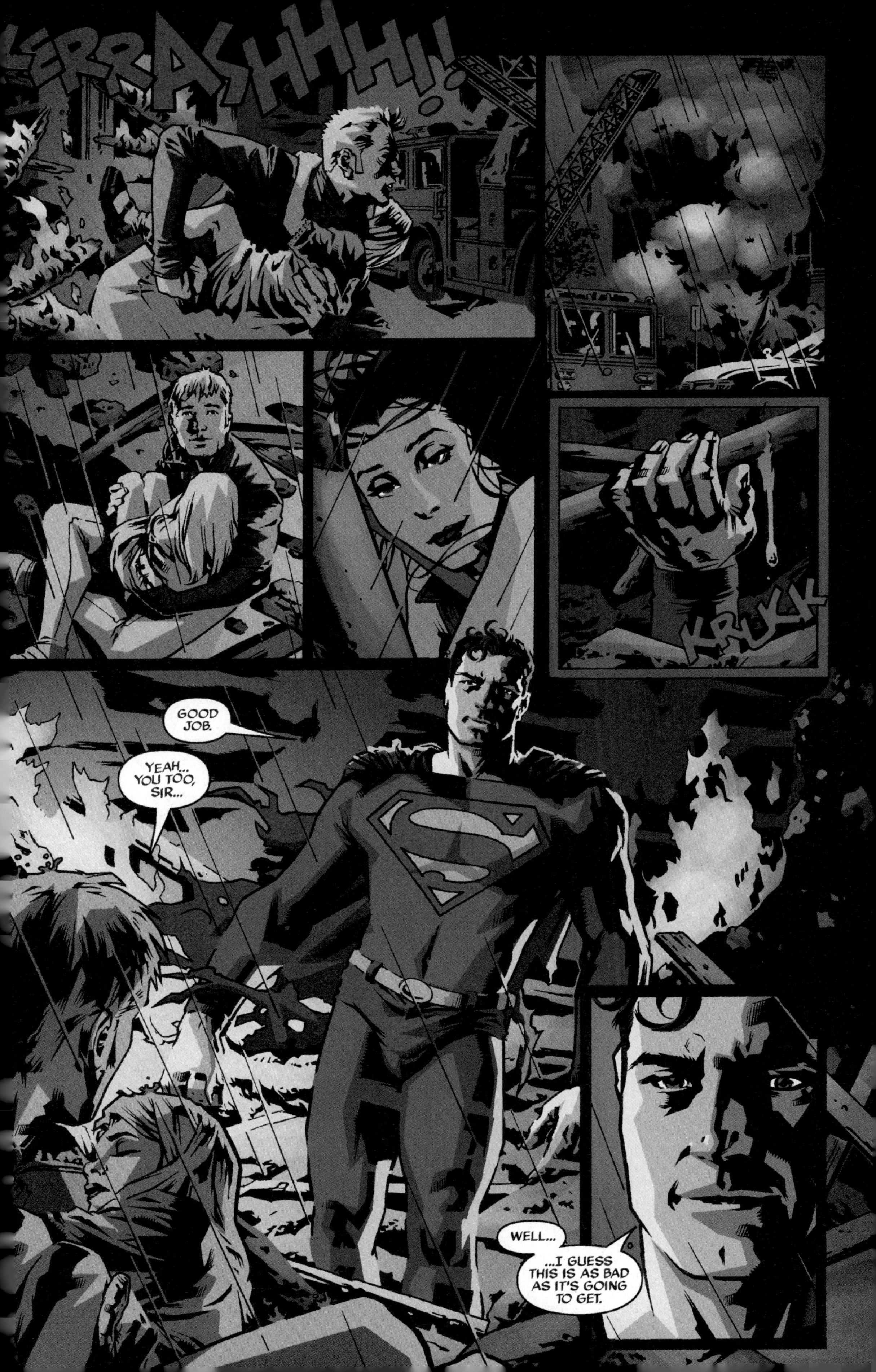
KRRASHHHH!!
KRUKK
GOOD JOB.
YEAH... YOU TOO, SIR...
WELL...
...I GUESS THIS IS AS BAD AS IT'S GOING TO GET.

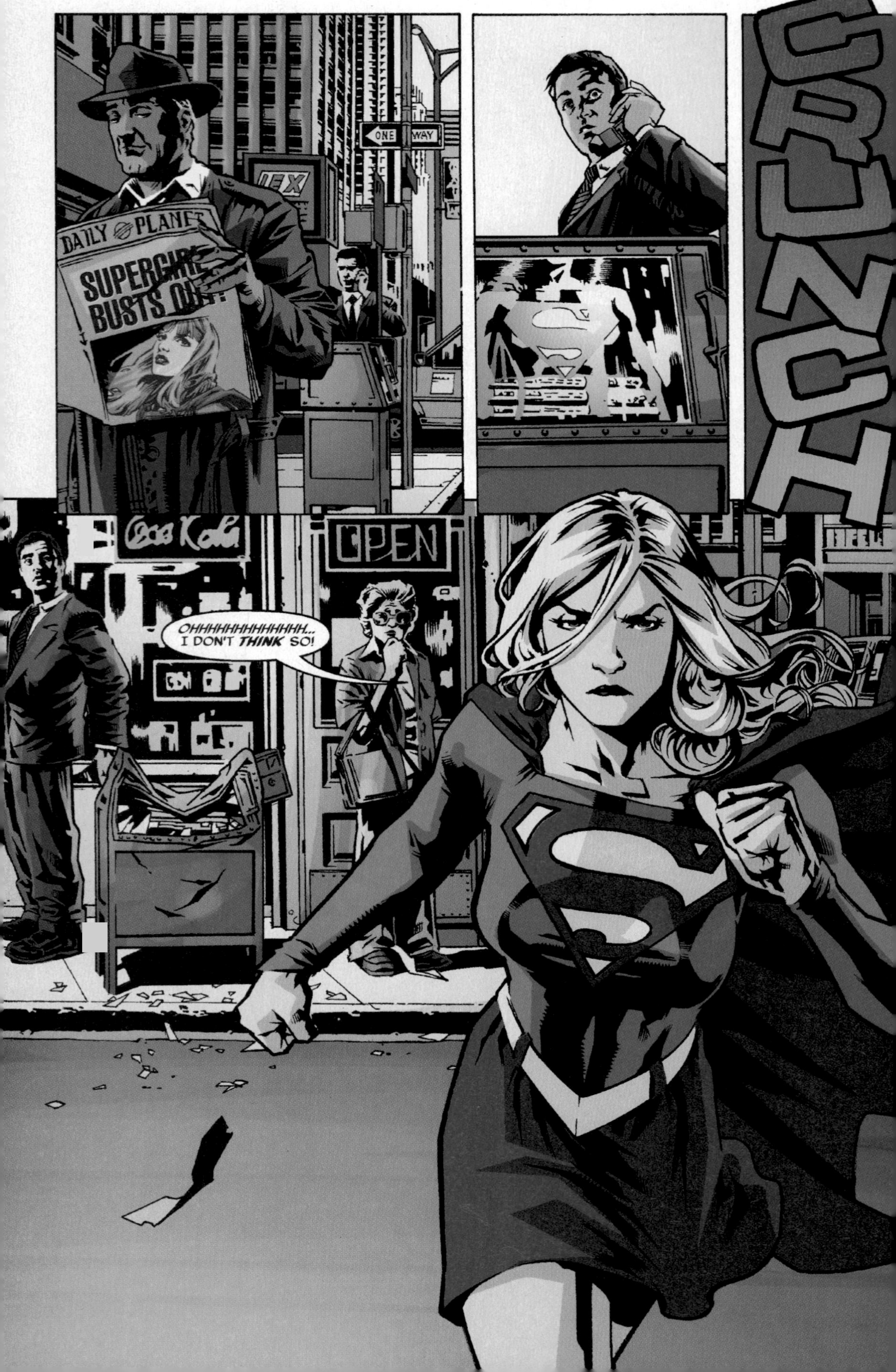
DAILY PLANET
SUPERGIRL BUSTS OUT!
ONE WAY
CRUNCH
OPEN
OHHHHHHHHHHHHHH... I DON'T THINK SO!

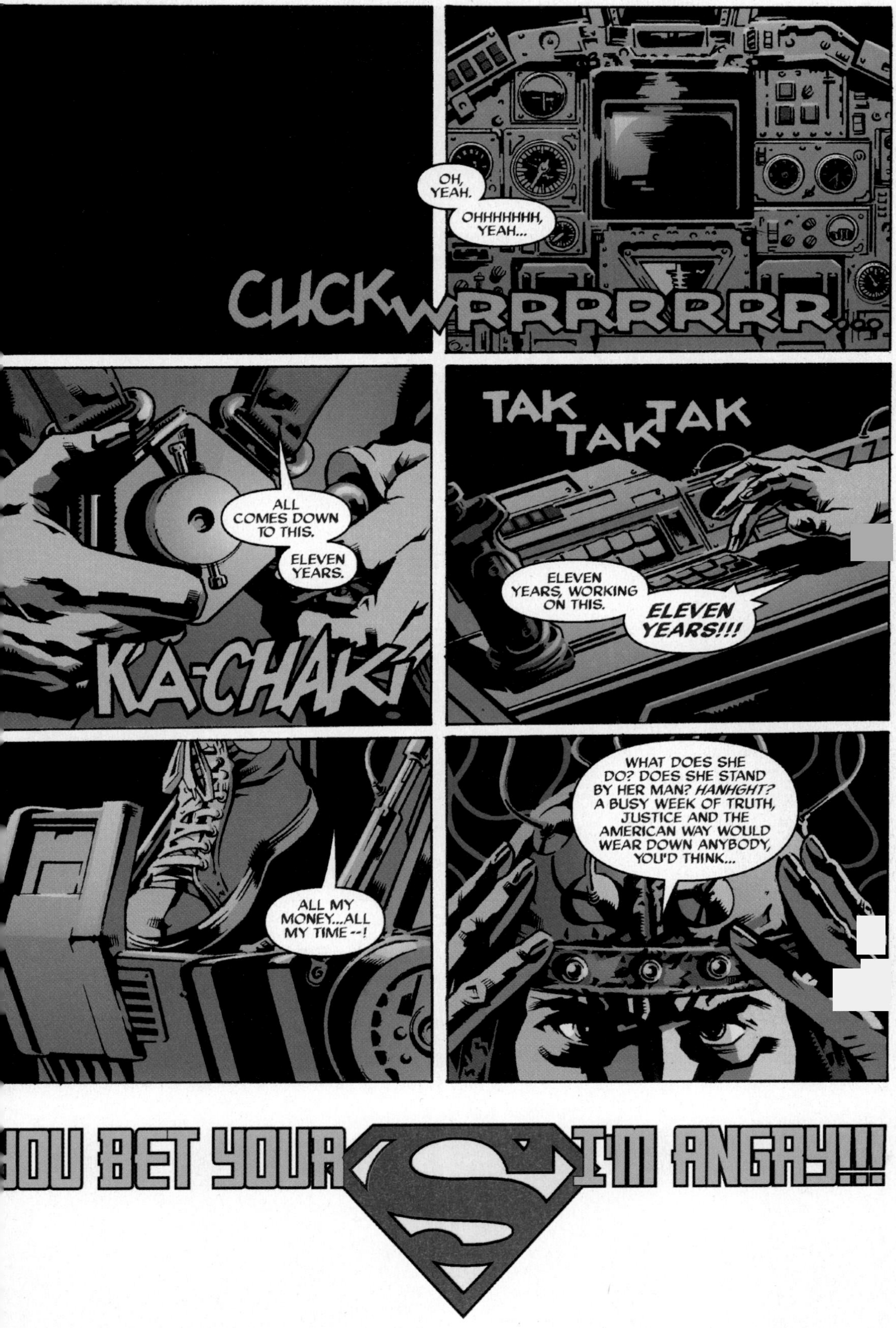
OH, YEAH.
OHHHHHHH, YEAH...
CLICK WRRRRRRR...
ALL COMES DOWN TO THIS.
ELEVEN YEARS.
KA-CHAK!
TAK TAK TAK
ELEVEN YEARS, WORKING ON THIS.
ELEVEN YEARS!!!
ALL MY MONEY...ALL MY TIME--!
WHAT DOES SHE DO? DOES SHE STAND BY HER MAN? HANHGHT? A BUSY WEEK OF TRUTH, JUSTICE AND THE AMERICAN WAY WOULD WEAR DOWN ANYBODY, YOU'D THINK...

YOU BET YOUR I'M ANGRY!!!

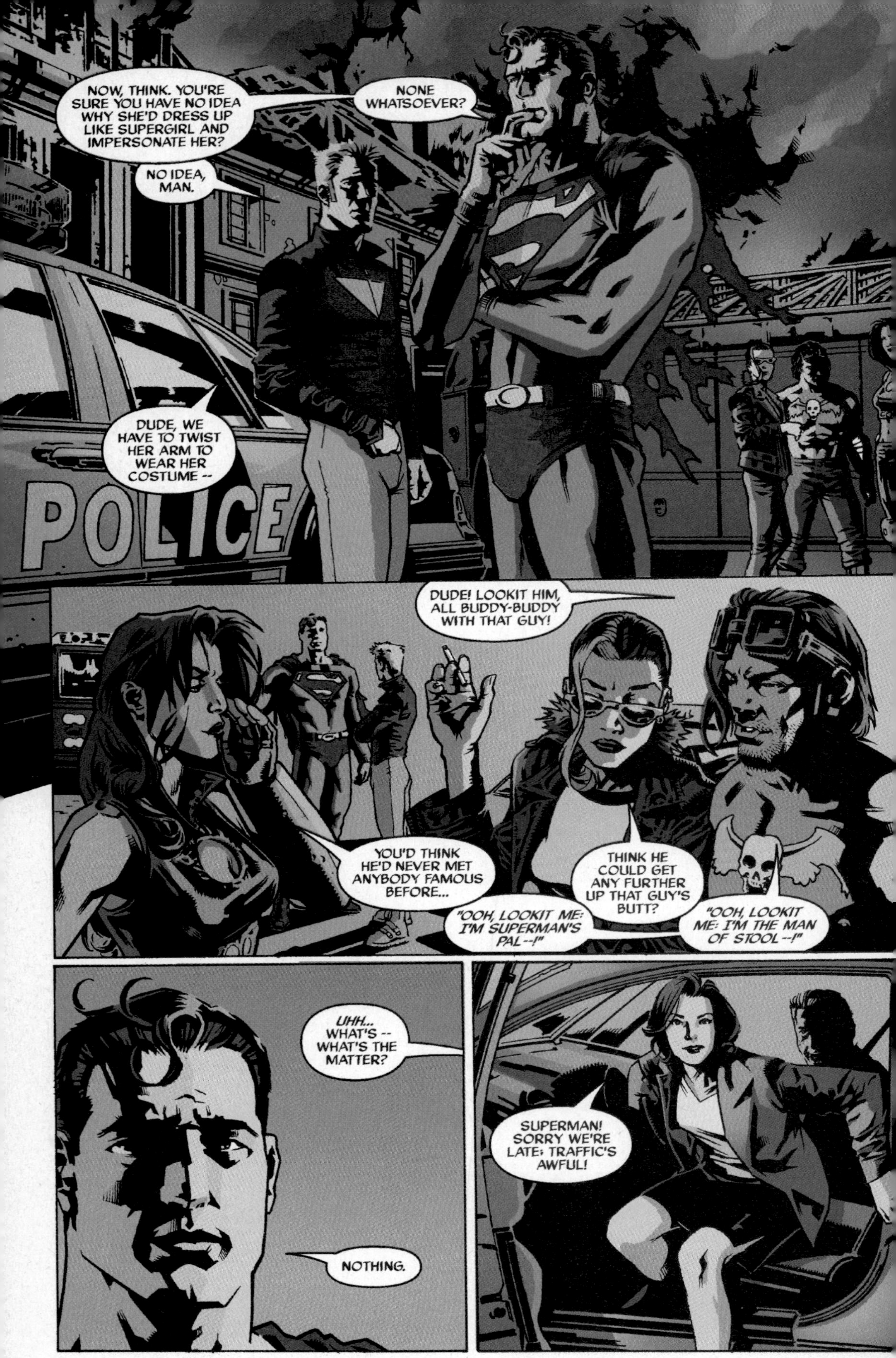
NOW, THINK. YOU'RE SURE YOU HAVE NO IDEA WHY SHE'D DRESS UP LIKE SUPERGIRL AND IMPERSONATE HER?
NONE WHATSOEVER?
NO IDEA, MAN.
DUDE, WE HAVE TO TWIST HER ARM TO WEAR HER COSTUME --
POLICE
DUDE! LOOKIT HIM, ALL BUDDY-BUDDY WITH THAT GUY!
YOU'D THINK HE'D NEVER MET ANYBODY FAMOUS BEFORE...
THINK HE COULD GET ANY FURTHER UP THAT GUY'S BUTT?
"OOH, LOOKIT ME: I'M SUPERMAN'S PAL--!"
"OOH, LOOKIT ME: I'M THE MAN OF STOOL--!"
UHH... WHAT'S -- WHAT'S THE MATTER?
NOTHING.
SUPERMAN! SORRY WE'RE LATE; TRAFFIC'S AWFUL!

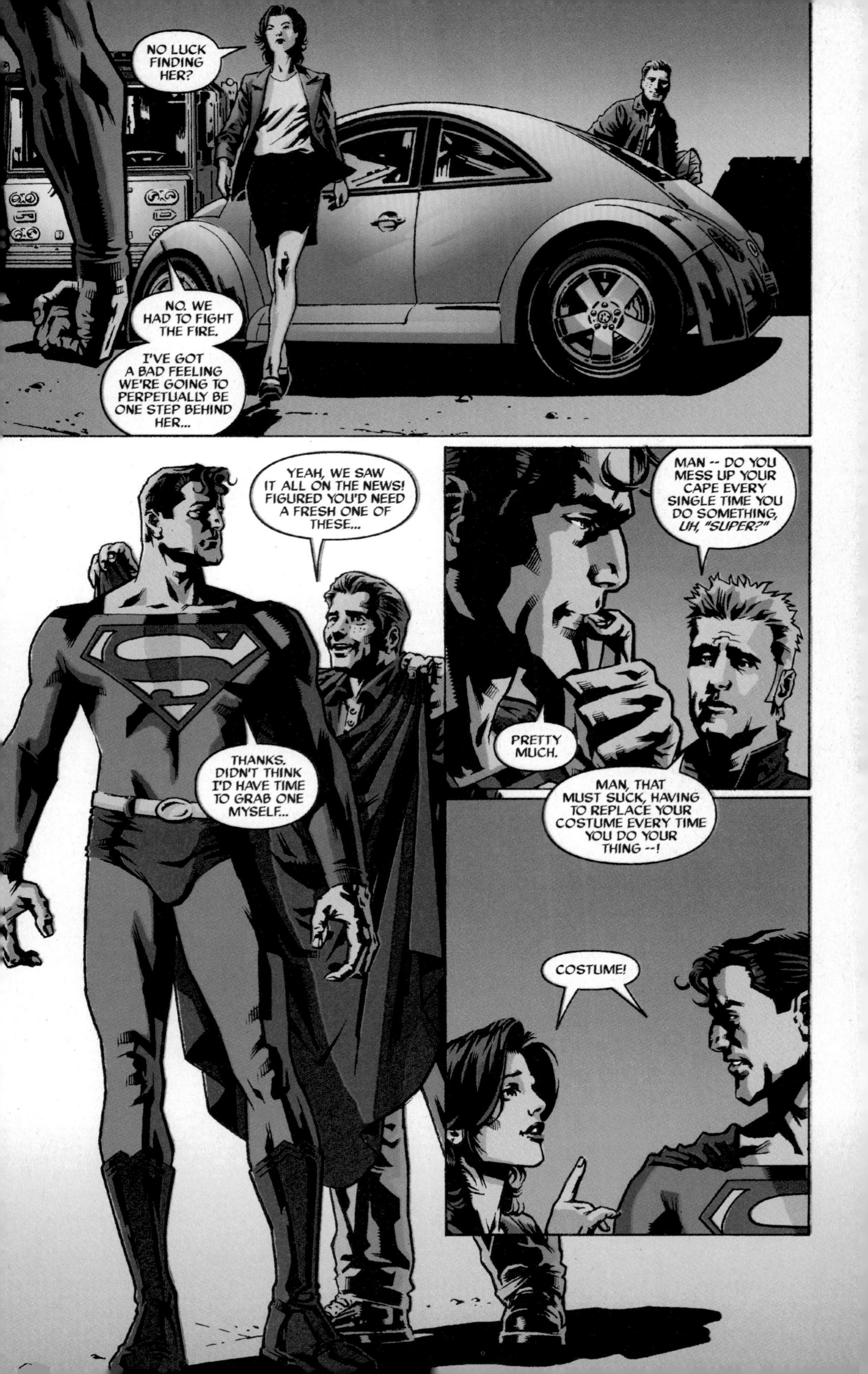
NO LUCK FINDING HER?
NO. WE HAD TO FIGHT THE FIRE.
I'VE GOT A BAD FEELING WE'RE GOING TO PERPETUALLY BE ONE STEP BEHIND HER...
YEAH, WE SAW IT ALL ON THE NEWS! FIGURED YOU'D NEED A FRESH ONE OF THESE...
THANKS. DIDN'T THINK I'D HAVE TIME TO GRAB ONE MYSELF...
MAN -- DO YOU MESS UP YOUR CAPE EVERY SINGLE TIME YOU DO SOMETHING, UH, "SUPER?"
PRETTY MUCH.
MAN, THAT MUST SUCK, HAVING TO REPLACE YOUR COSTUME EVERY TIME YOU DO YOUR THING --!
COSTUME!

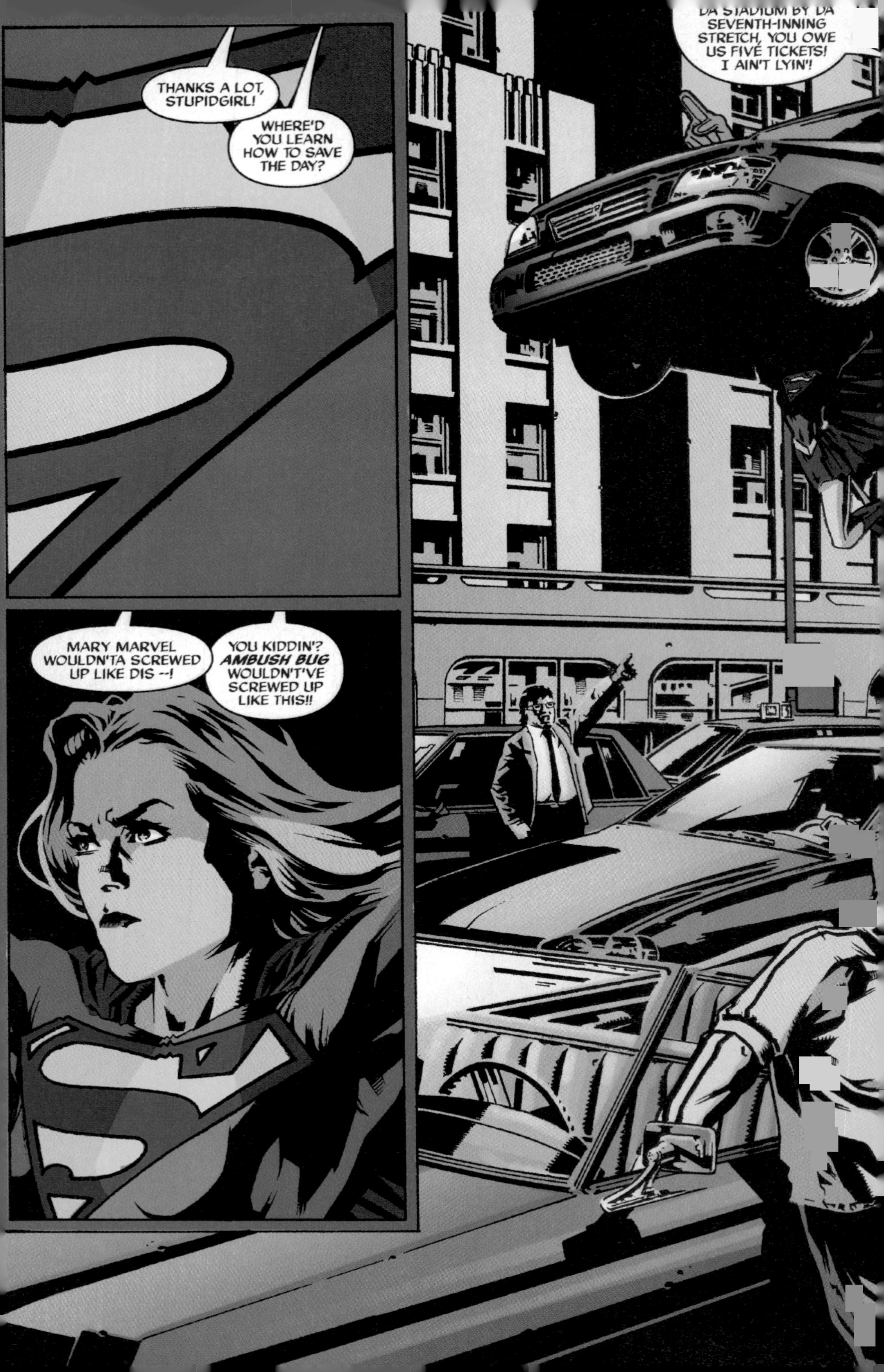
DA STADIUM BY DA SEVENTH-INNING STRETCH, YOU OWE US FIVE TICKETS! I AIN'T LYIN'!
THANKS A LOT, STUPIDGIRL!
WHERE'D YOU LEARN HOW TO SAVE THE DAY?
MARY MARVEL WOULDN'TA SCREWED UP LIKE DIS --!
YOU KIDDIN'? AMBUSH BUG WOULDN'T'VE SCREWED UP LIKE THIS!!

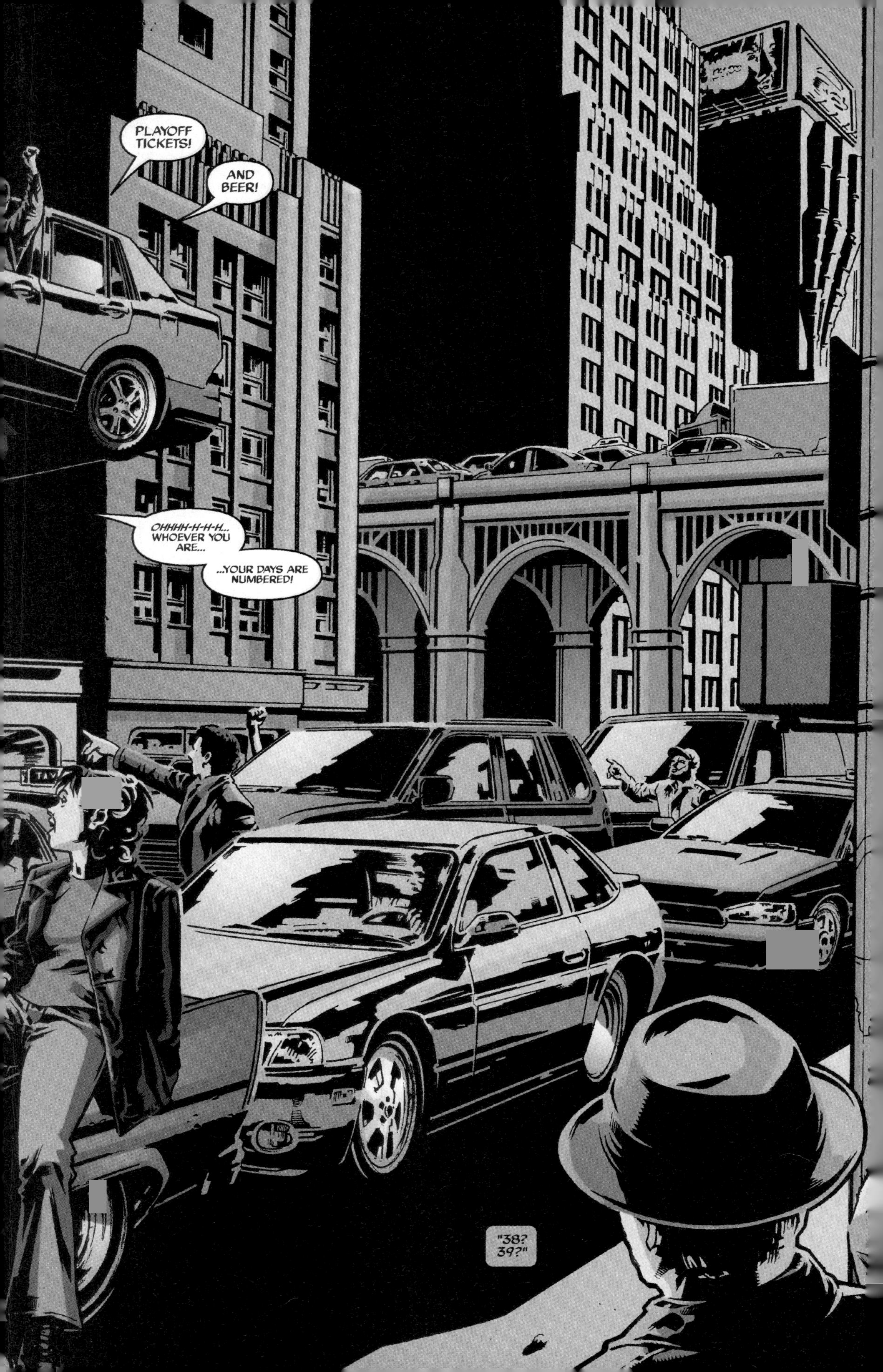
PLAYOFF TICKETS!
AND BEER!
OHHHH-H-H-H... WHOEVER YOU ARE...
...YOUR DAYS ARE NUMBERED!
"38? 39?"

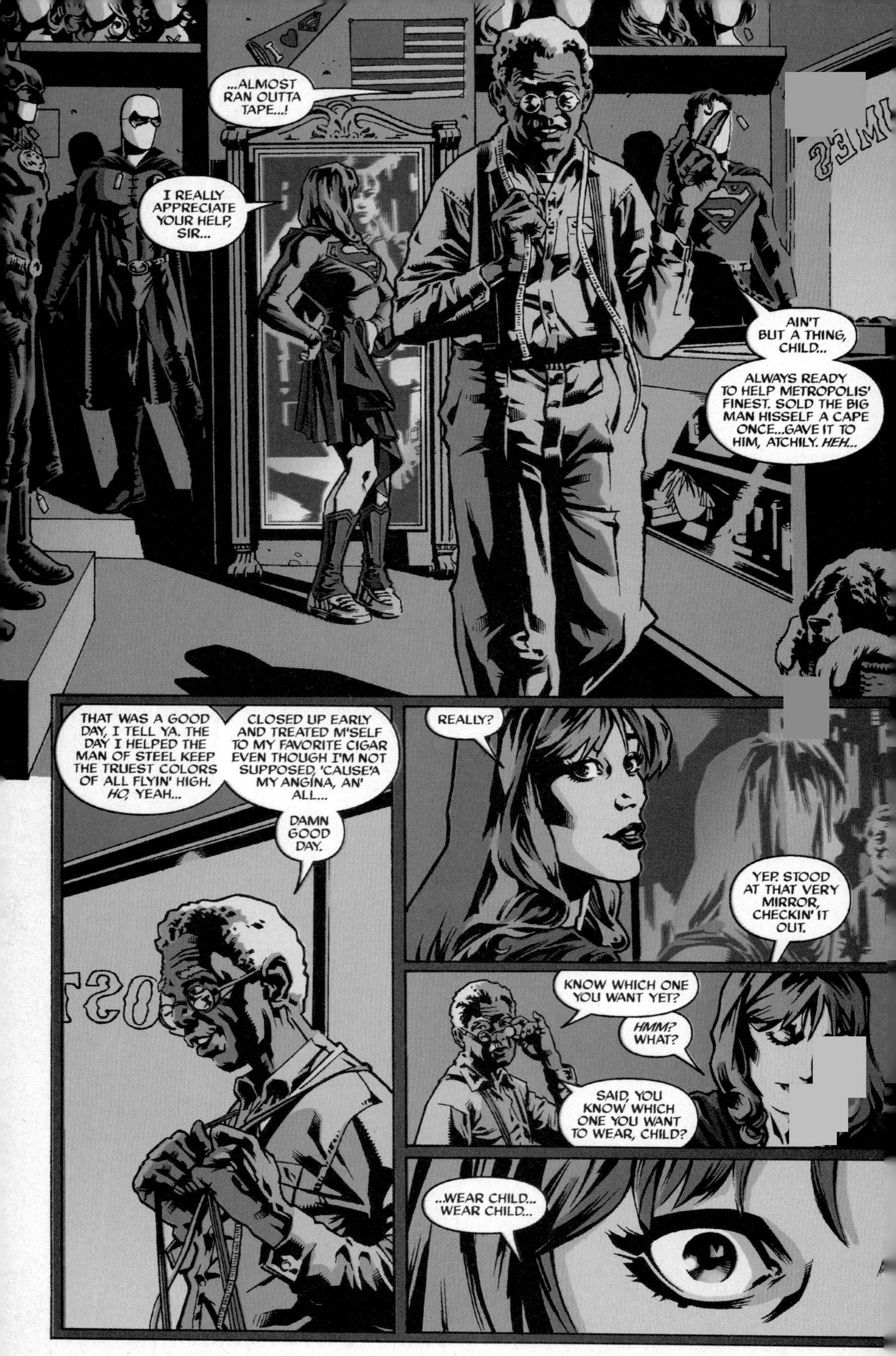

...ALMOST RAN OUTTA TAPE...!
I REALLY APPRECIATE YOUR HELP, SIR...
AIN'T BUT A THING, CHILD...
ALWAYS READY TO HELP METROPOLIS' FINEST. SOLD THE BIG MAN HISSELF A CAPE ONCE...GAVE IT TO HIM, ATCHILY. *HEH...*
THAT WAS A GOOD DAY, I TELL YA. THE DAY I HELPED THE MAN OF STEEL KEEP THE TRUEST COLORS OF ALL FLYIN' HIGH. *HO,* YEAH...
CLOSED UP EARLY AND TREATED M'SELF TO MY FAVORITE CIGAR EVEN THOUGH I'M NOT SUPPOSED, 'CAUSE'A MY ANGINA, AN' ALL...
DAMN GOOD DAY.
REALLY?
YEP, STOOD AT THAT VERY MIRROR, CHECKIN' IT OUT.
KNOW WHICH ONE YOU WANT YET?
HMM? WHAT?
SAID, YOU KNOW WHICH ONE YOU WANT TO WEAR, CHILD?
...WEAR CHILD... WEAR CHILD...

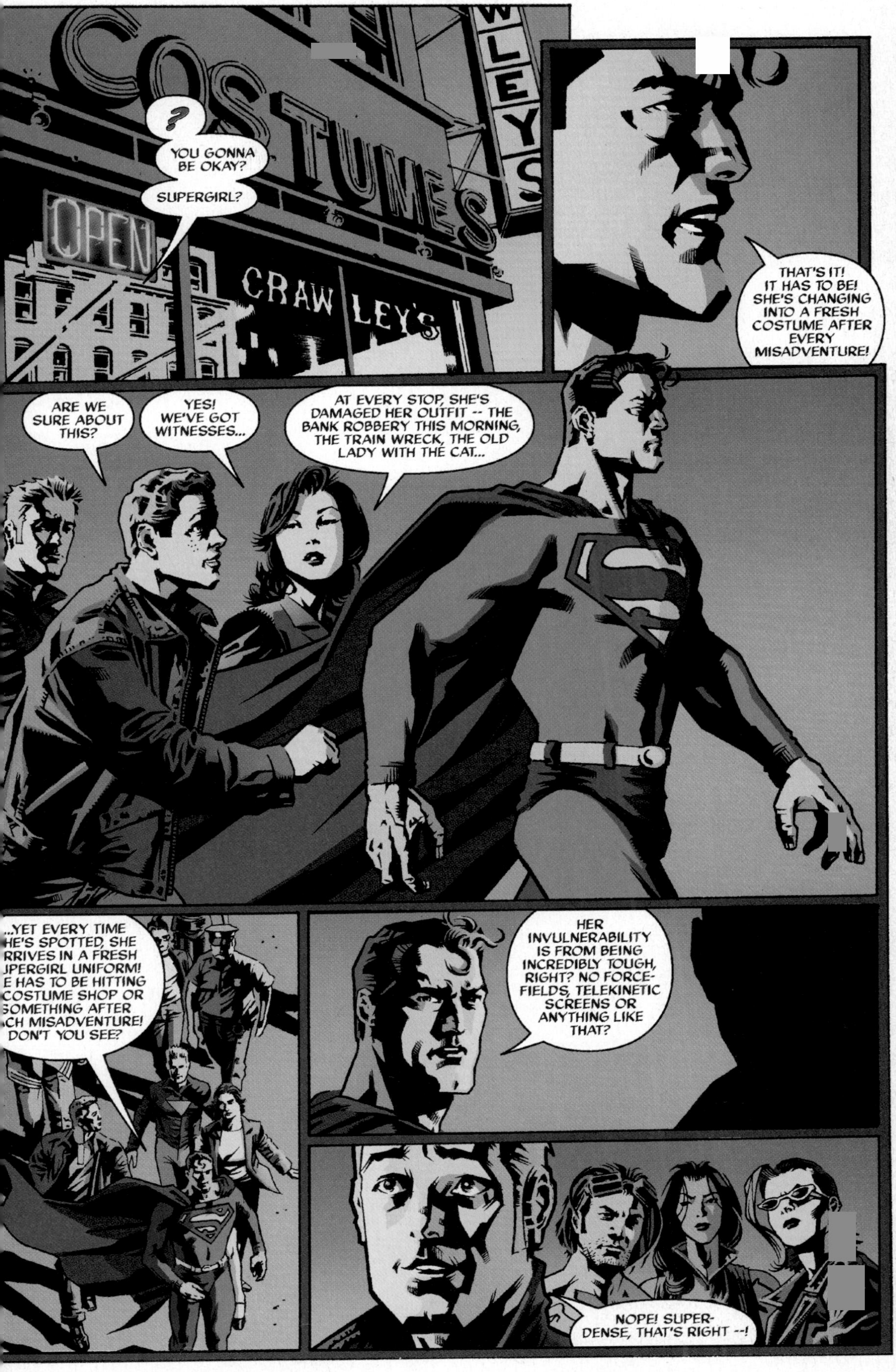

?
YOU GONNA BE OKAY?
SUPERGIRL?
COSTUMES
OPEN
CRAWLEY'S
THAT'S IT! IT HAS TO BE! SHE'S CHANGING INTO A FRESH COSTUME AFTER EVERY MISADVENTURE!
ARE WE SURE ABOUT THIS?
YES! WE'VE GOT WITNESSES...
AT EVERY STOP, SHE'S DAMAGED HER OUTFIT -- THE BANK ROBBERY THIS MORNING, THE TRAIN WRECK, THE OLD LADY WITH THE CAT...
...YET EVERY TIME HE'S SPOTTED, SHE RRIVES IN A FRESH UPERGIRL UNIFORM! E HAS TO BE HITTING COSTUME SHOP OR SOMETHING AFTER CH MISADVENTURE! DON'T YOU SEE?
HER INVULNERABILITY IS FROM BEING INCREDIBLY TOUGH, RIGHT? NO FORCE-FIELDS, TELEKINETIC SCREENS OR ANYTHING LIKE THAT?
NOPE! SUPER-DENSE, THAT'S RIGHT --!

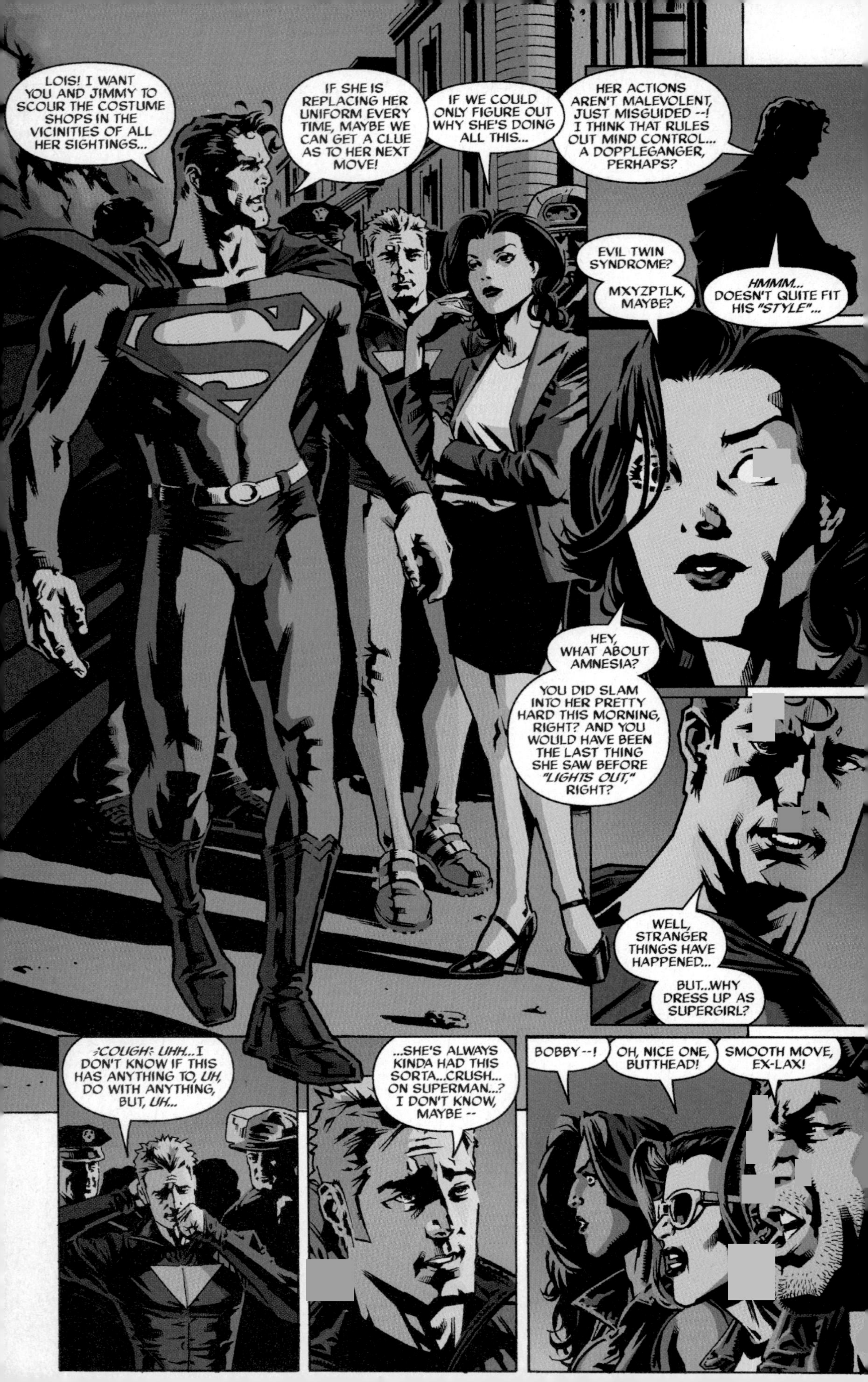
LOIS! I WANT YOU AND JIMMY TO SCOUR THE COSTUME SHOPS IN THE VICINITIES OF ALL HER SIGHTINGS...
IF SHE IS REPLACING HER UNIFORM EVERY TIME, MAYBE WE CAN GET A CLUE AS TO HER NEXT MOVE!
IF WE COULD ONLY FIGURE OUT WHY SHE'S DOING ALL THIS...
HER ACTIONS AREN'T MALEVOLENT, JUST MISGUIDED --! I THINK THAT RULES OUT MIND CONTROL... A DOPPLEGANGER, PERHAPS?
EVIL TWIN SYNDROME?
MXYZPTLK, MAYBE?
HMMM... DOESN'T QUITE FIT HIS *"STYLE"*...
HEY, WHAT ABOUT AMNESIA?
YOU DID SLAM INTO HER PRETTY HARD THIS MORNING, RIGHT? AND YOU WOULD HAVE BEEN THE LAST THING SHE SAW BEFORE *"LIGHTS OUT,"* RIGHT?
WELL, STRANGER THINGS HAVE HAPPENED...
BUT...WHY DRESS UP AS SUPERGIRL?
:COUGH: *UHH*...I DON'T KNOW IF THIS HAS ANYTHING TO, *UH*, DO WITH ANYTHING, BUT, *UH*...
...SHE'S ALWAYS KINDA HAD THIS SORTA...CRUSH... ON SUPERMAN...? I DON'T KNOW, MAYBE --
BOBBY --!
OH, NICE ONE, BUTTHEAD!
SMOOTH MOVE, EX-LAX!

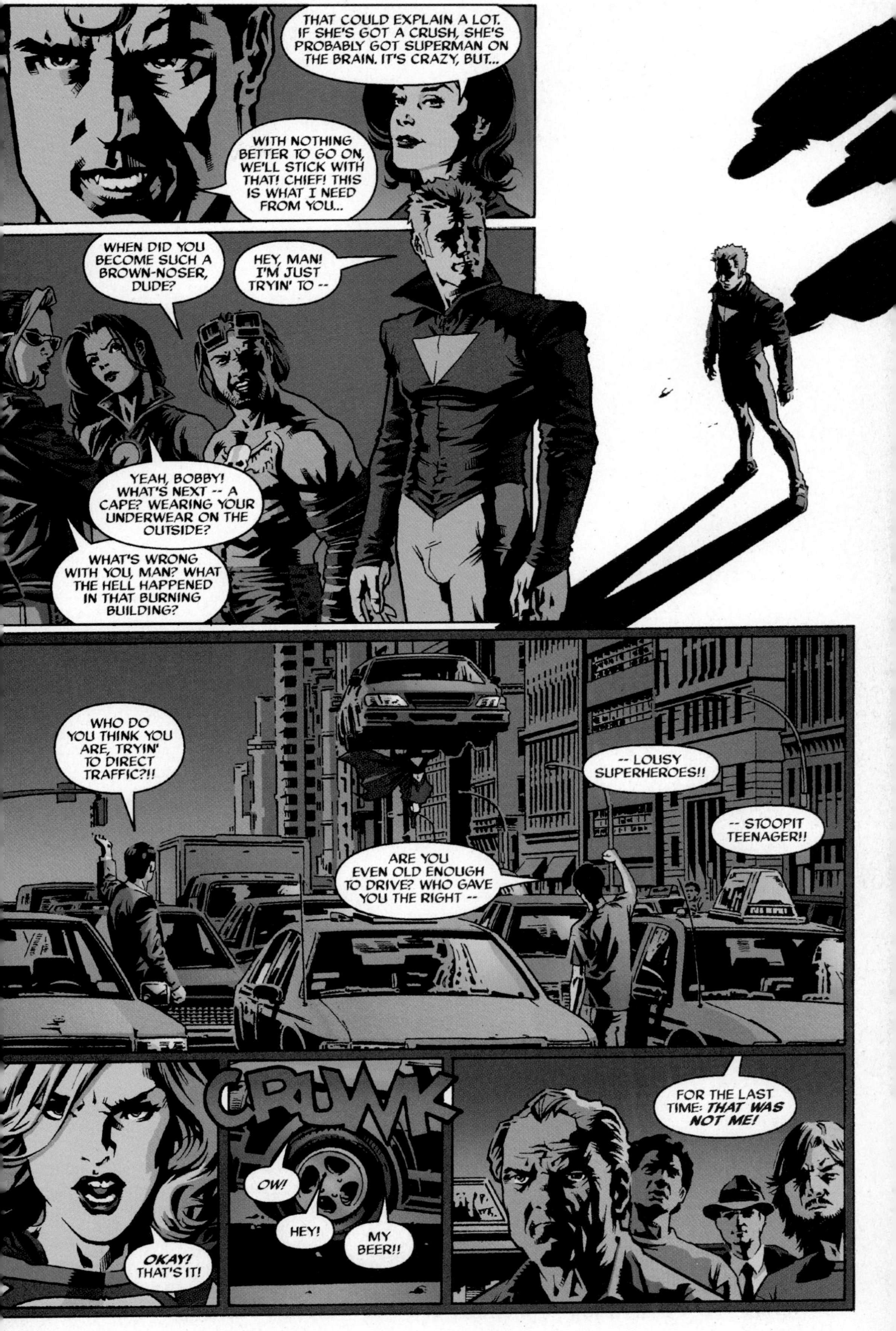
THAT COULD EXPLAIN A LOT. IF SHE'S GOT A CRUSH, SHE'S PROBABLY GOT SUPERMAN ON THE BRAIN. IT'S CRAZY, BUT...
WITH NOTHING BETTER TO GO ON, WE'LL STICK WITH THAT! CHIEF! THIS IS WHAT I NEED FROM YOU...
WHEN DID YOU BECOME SUCH A BROWN-NOSER, DUDE?
HEY, MAN! I'M JUST TRYIN' TO --
YEAH, BOBBY! WHAT'S NEXT -- A CAPE? WEARING YOUR UNDERWEAR ON THE OUTSIDE?
WHAT'S WRONG WITH YOU, MAN? WHAT THE HELL HAPPENED IN THAT BURNING BUILDING?
WHO DO YOU THINK YOU ARE, TRYIN' TO DIRECT TRAFFIC?!!
-- LOUSY SUPERHEROES!!
ARE YOU EVEN OLD ENOUGH TO DRIVE? WHO GAVE YOU THE RIGHT --
-- STOOPIT TEENAGER!!
OKAY! THAT'S IT!
CRUNK
OW!
HEY!
MY BEER!!
FOR THE LAST TIME: THAT WAS NOT ME!

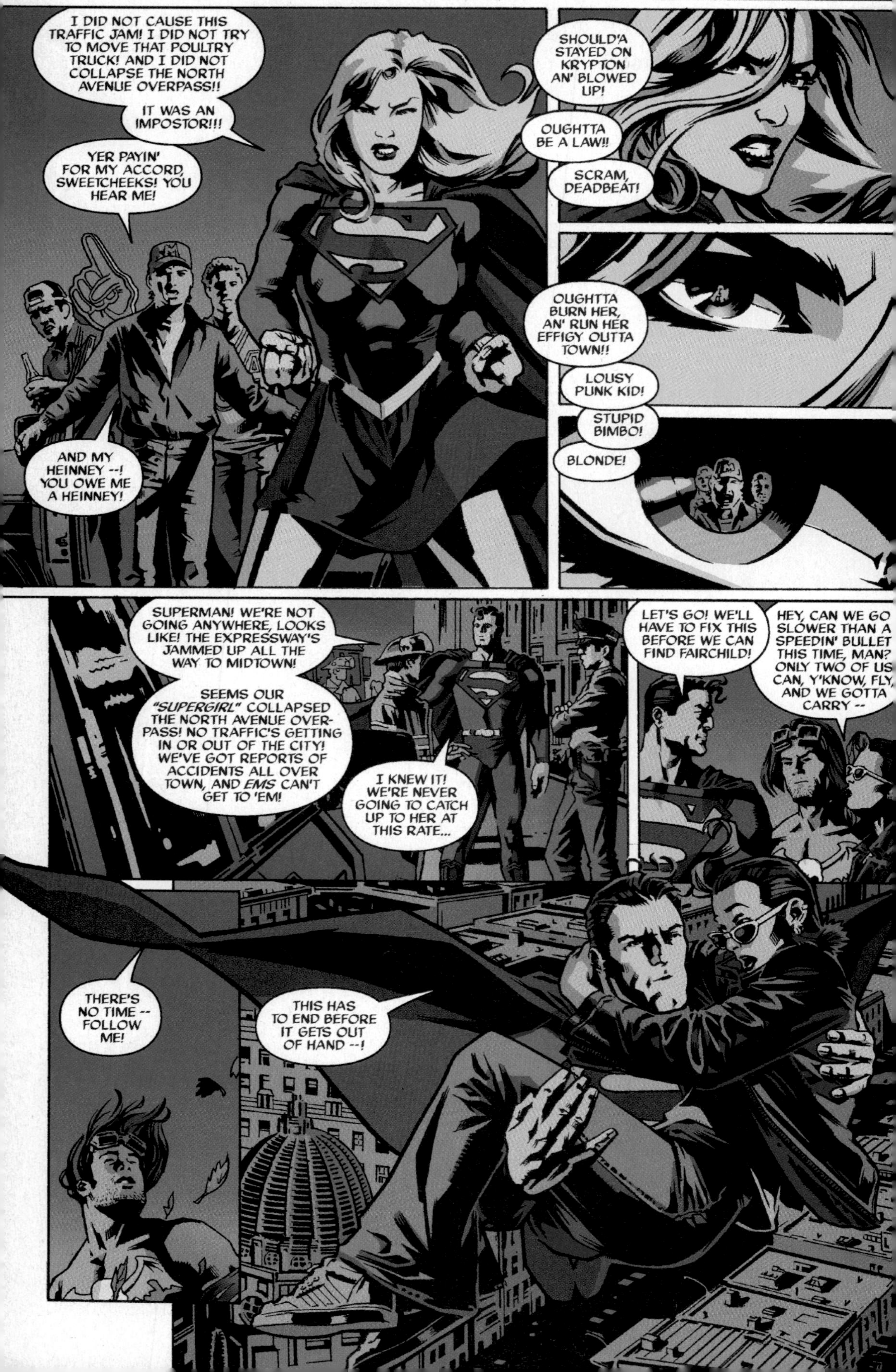

I DID NOT CAUSE THIS TRAFFIC JAM! I DID NOT TRY TO MOVE THAT POULTRY TRUCK! AND I DID NOT COLLAPSE THE NORTH AVENUE OVERPASS!!
IT WAS AN IMPOSTOR!!!
YER PAYIN' FOR MY ACCORD, SWEETCHEEKS! YOU HEAR ME!
AND MY HEINNEY --! YOU OWE ME A HEINNEY!
SHOULD'A STAYED ON KRYPTON AN' BLOWED UP!
OUGHTTA BE A LAW!!
SCRAM, DEADBEAT!
OUGHTTA BURN HER, AN' RUN HER EFFIGY OUTTA TOWN!!
LOUSY PUNK KID!
STUPID BIMBO!
BLONDE!
SUPERMAN! WE'RE NOT GOING ANYWHERE, LOOKS LIKE! THE EXPRESSWAY'S JAMMED UP ALL THE WAY TO MIDTOWN!
SEEMS OUR "SUPERGIRL" COLLAPSED THE NORTH AVENUE OVER-PASS! NO TRAFFIC'S GETTING IN OR OUT OF THE CITY! WE'VE GOT REPORTS OF ACCIDENTS ALL OVER TOWN, AND EMS CAN'T GET TO 'EM!
I KNEW IT! WE'RE NEVER GOING TO CATCH UP TO HER AT THIS RATE...
LET'S GO! WE'LL HAVE TO FIX THIS BEFORE WE CAN FIND FAIRCHILD!
HEY, CAN WE GO SLOWER THAN A SPEEDIN' BULLET THIS TIME, MAN? ONLY TWO OF US CAN, Y'KNOW, FLY, AND WE GOTTA CARRY --
THERE'S NO TIME -- FOLLOW ME!
THIS HAS TO END BEFORE IT GETS OUT OF HAND --!

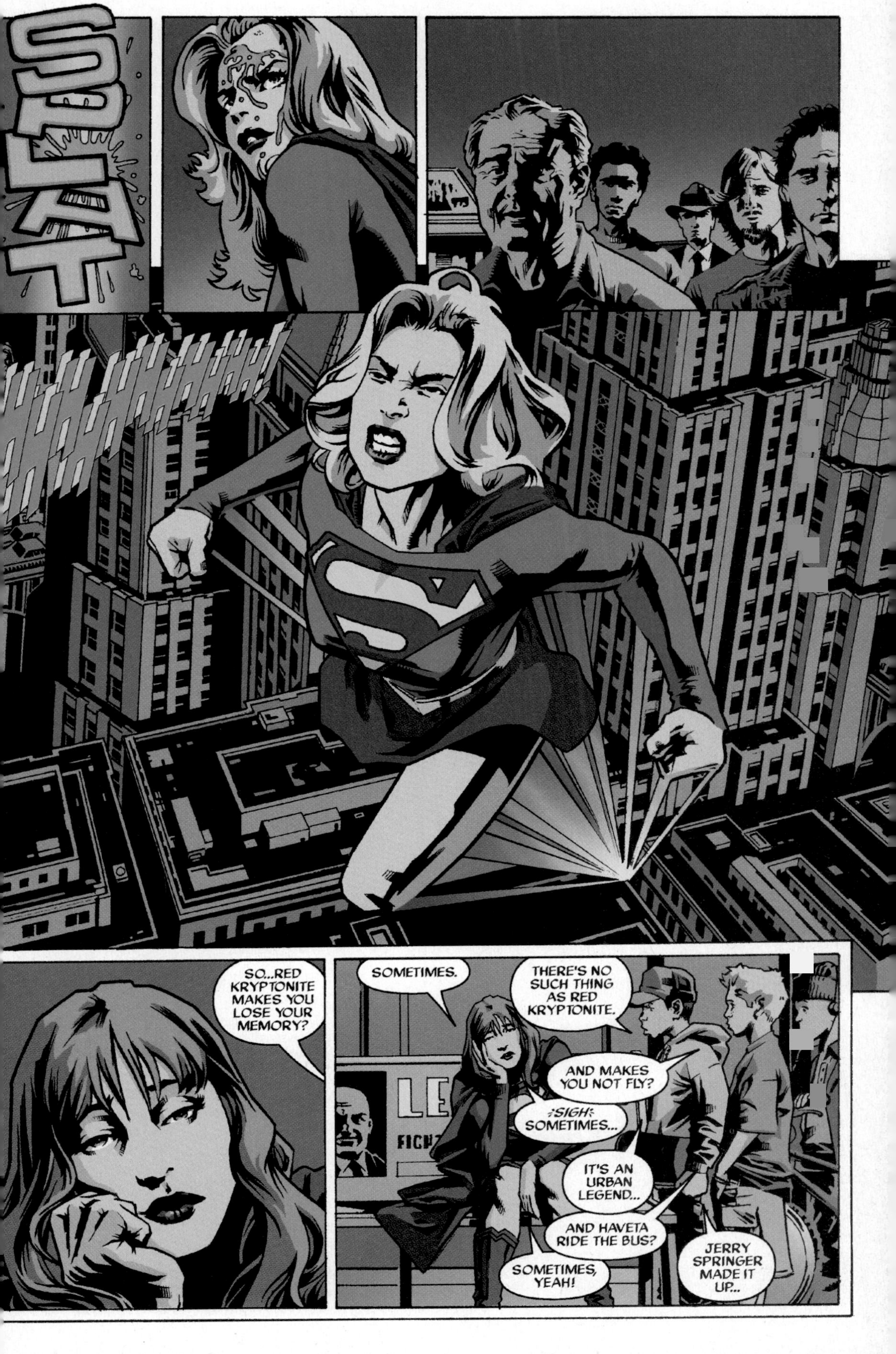
SPLAT
HAHHAHHAHHAHHAH!
SO...RED KRYPTONITE MAKES YOU LOSE YOUR MEMORY?
SOMETIMES.
THERE'S NO SUCH THING AS RED KRYPTONITE.
AND MAKES YOU NOT FLY?
SIGH SOMETIMES...
IT'S AN URBAN LEGEND...
AND HAVETA RIDE THE BUS?
SOMETIMES, YEAH!
JERRY SPRINGER MADE IT UP...

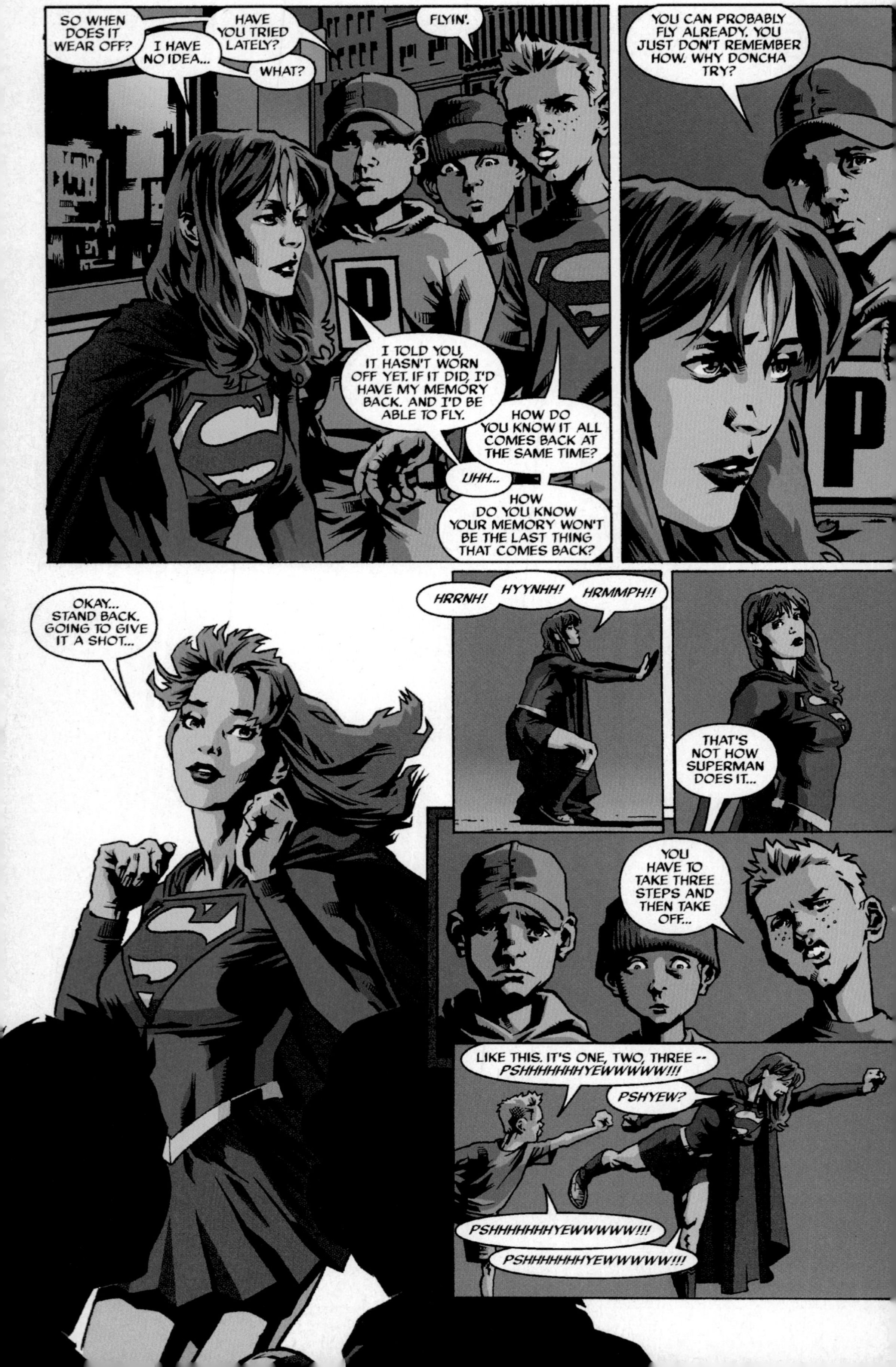
SO WHEN DOES IT WEAR OFF?
I HAVE NO IDEA...
HAVE YOU TRIED LATELY?
WHAT?
FLYIN'.
I TOLD YOU, IT HASN'T WORN OFF YET. IF IT DID, I'D HAVE MY MEMORY BACK. AND I'D BE ABLE TO FLY.
HOW DO YOU KNOW IT ALL COMES BACK AT THE SAME TIME?
UHH...
HOW DO YOU KNOW YOUR MEMORY WON'T BE THE LAST THING THAT COMES BACK?
YOU CAN PROBABLY FLY ALREADY. YOU JUST DON'T REMEMBER HOW. WHY DONCHA TRY?
OKAY... STAND BACK. GOING TO GIVE IT A SHOT...
HRRNH!
HYYNHH!
HRMMPH!!
THAT'S NOT HOW SUPERMAN DOES IT...
YOU HAVE TO TAKE THREE STEPS AND THEN TAKE OFF...
LIKE THIS. IT'S ONE, TWO, THREE -- PSHHHHHHHYEWWWWW!!!
PSHYEW?
PSHHHHHHHYEWWWWW!!!
PSHHHHHHHYEWWWWW!!!

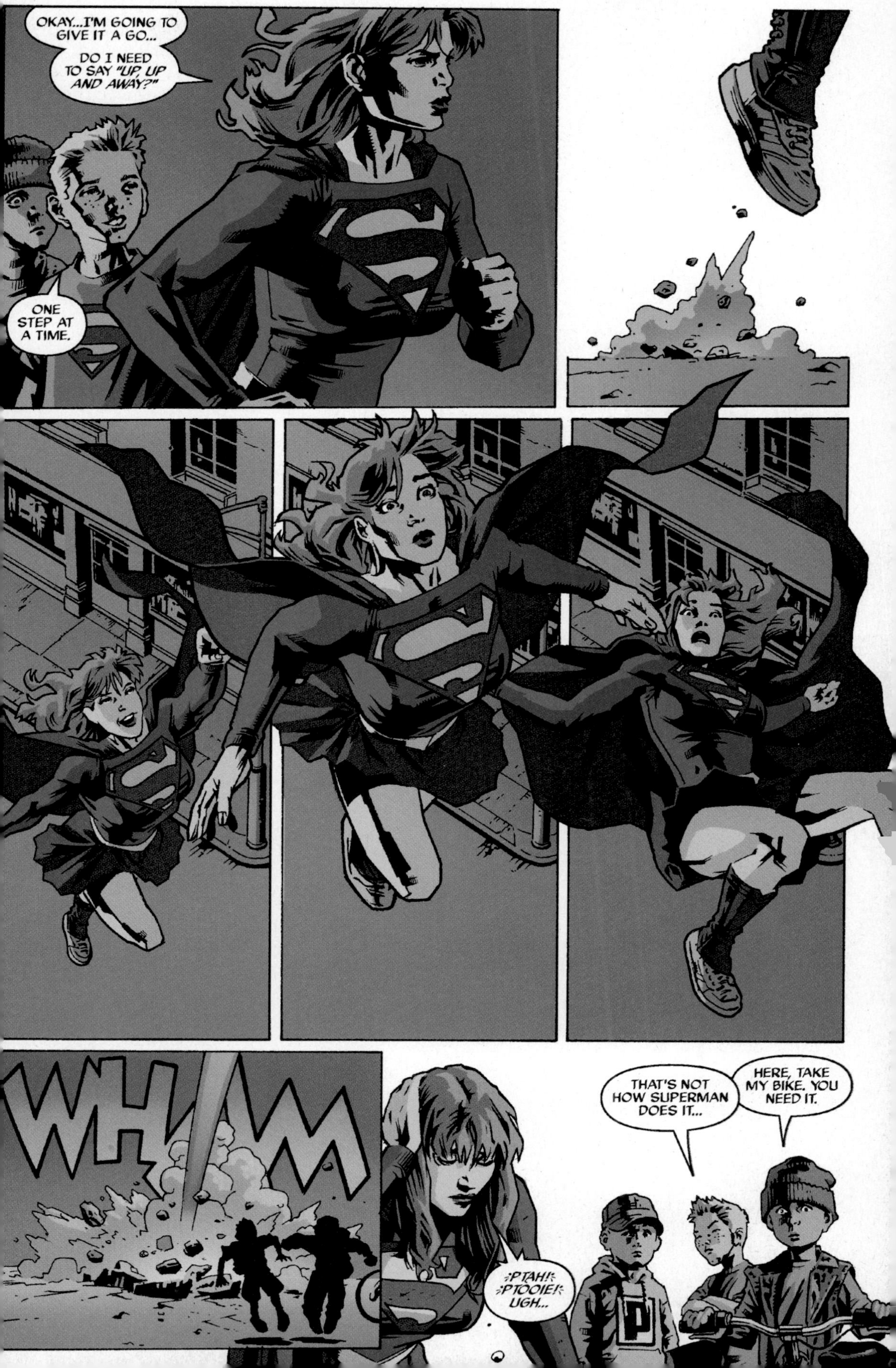
OKAY...I'M GOING TO GIVE IT A GO...
DO I NEED TO SAY "UP, UP AND AWAY?"
ONE STEP AT A TIME.
WHAM
PTAH! PTOOIE! UGH...
THAT'S NOT HOW SUPERMAN DOES IT...
HERE, TAKE MY BIKE. YOU NEED IT.

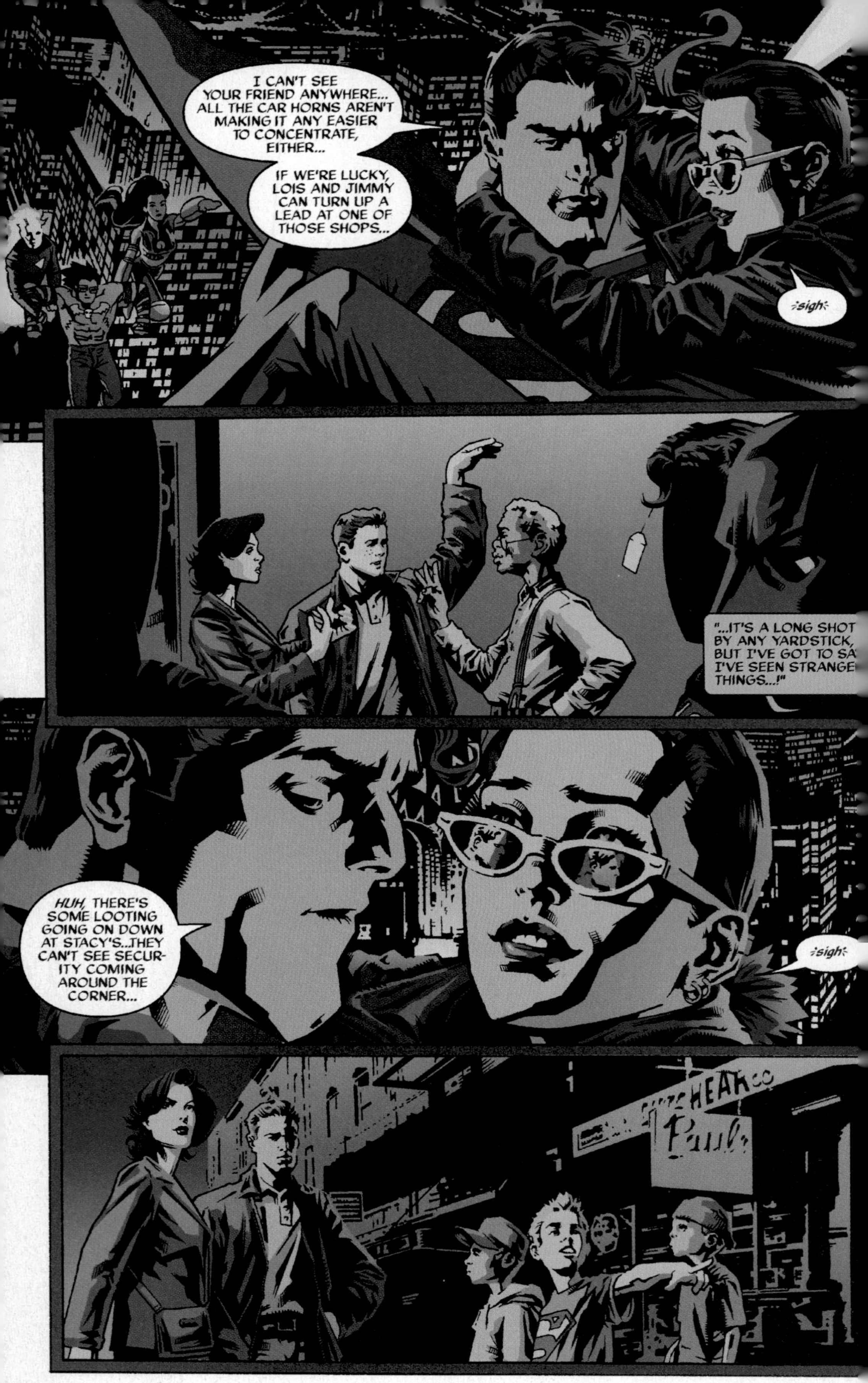
I CAN'T SEE YOUR FRIEND ANYWHERE... ALL THE CAR HORNS AREN'T MAKING IT ANY EASIER TO CONCENTRATE, EITHER...
IF WE'RE LUCKY, LOIS AND JIMMY CAN TURN UP A LEAD AT ONE OF THOSE SHOPS...
sigh
"...IT'S A LONG SHOT BY ANY YARDSTICK, BUT I'VE GOT TO SA I'VE SEEN STRANGE THINGS...!"
HUH, THERE'S SOME LOOTING GOING ON DOWN AT STACY'S...THEY CAN'T SEE SECURITY COMING AROUND THE CORNER...
sigh

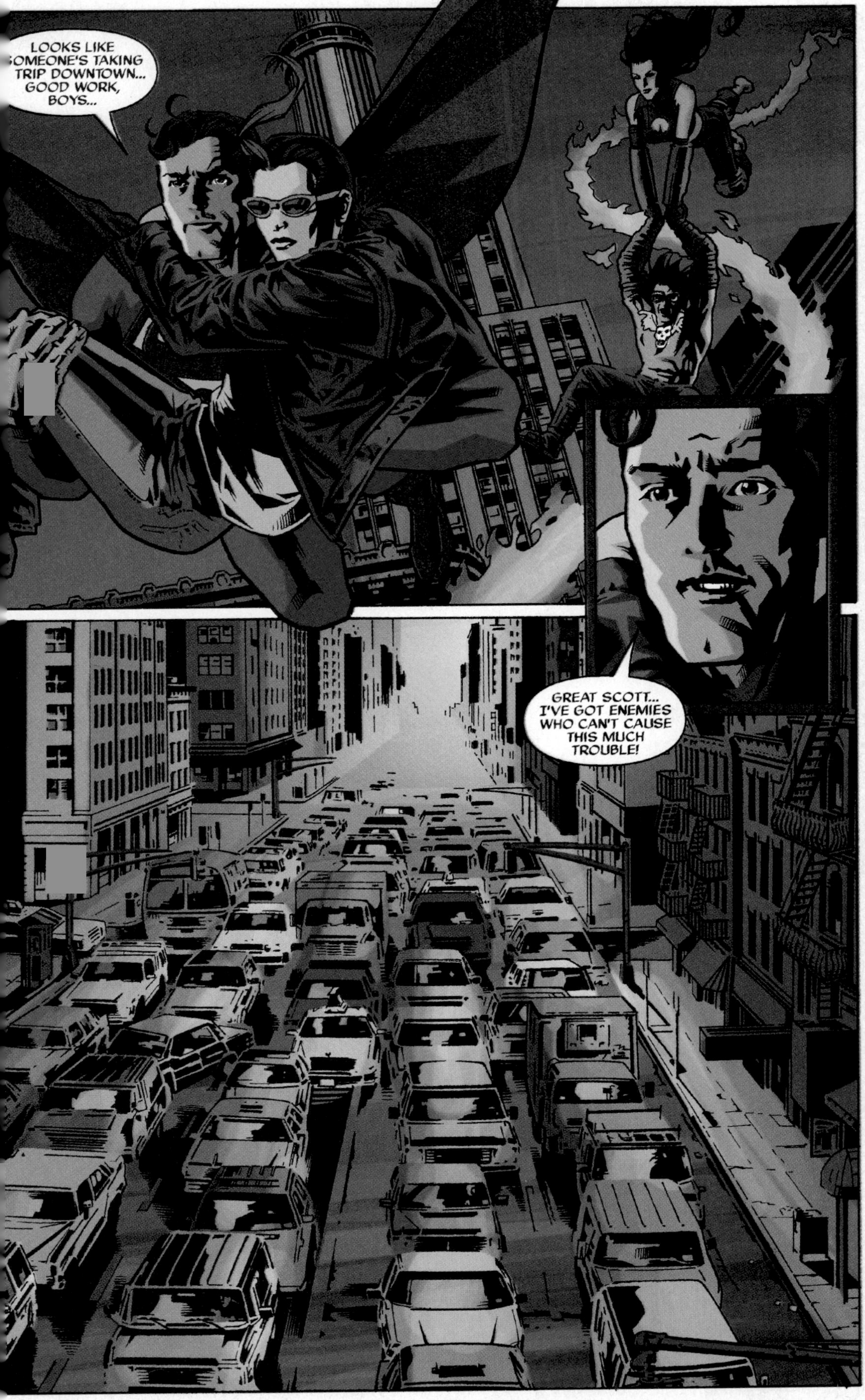
LOOKS LIKE SOMEONE'S TAKING TRIP DOWNTOWN... GOOD WORK, BOYS...
GREAT SCOTT... I'VE GOT ENEMIES WHO CAN'T CAUSE THIS MUCH TROUBLE!

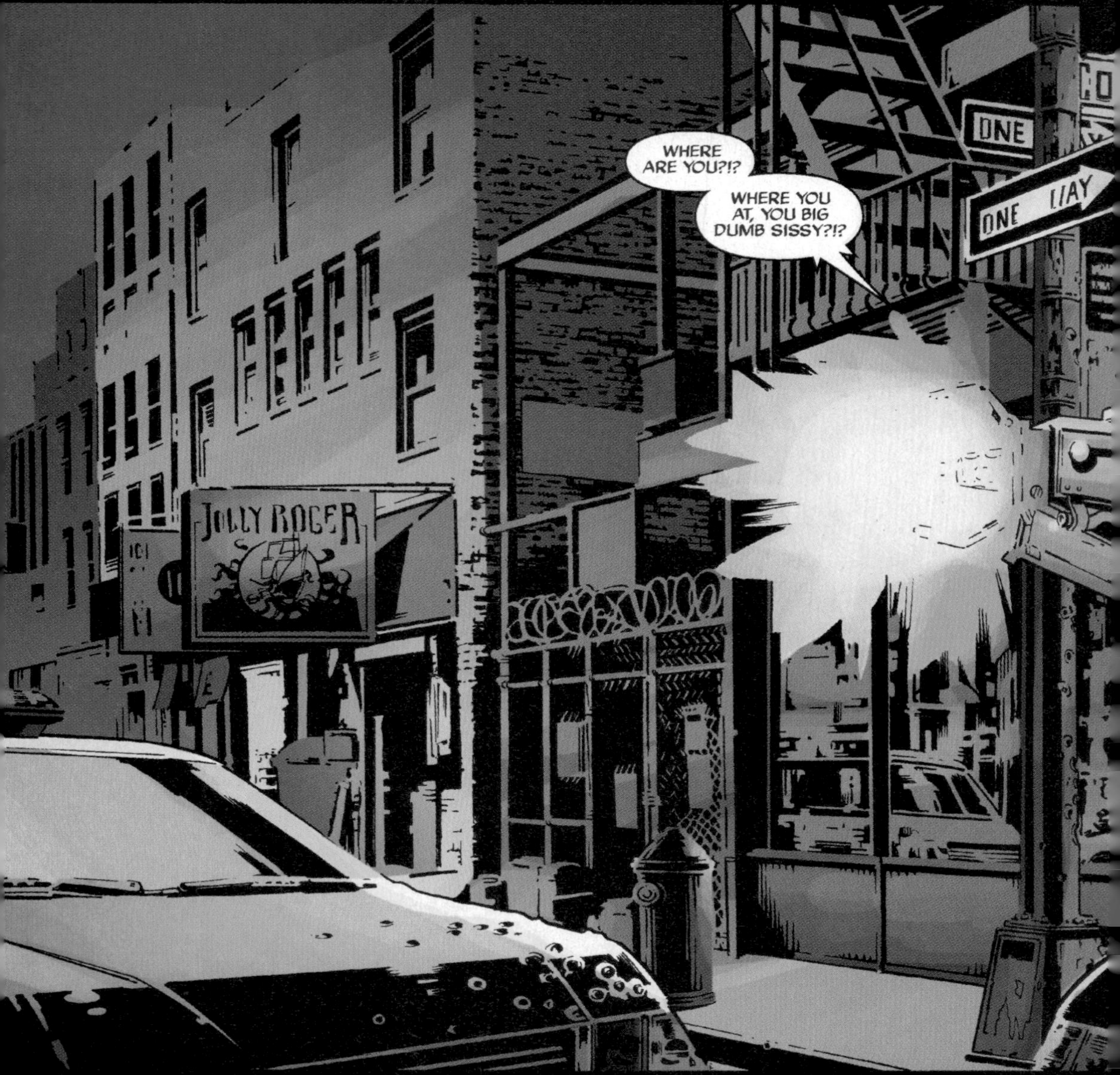
WHERE ARE YOU?!?
WHERE YOU AT, YOU BIG DUMB SISSY?!?
JOLLY ROGER
ONE

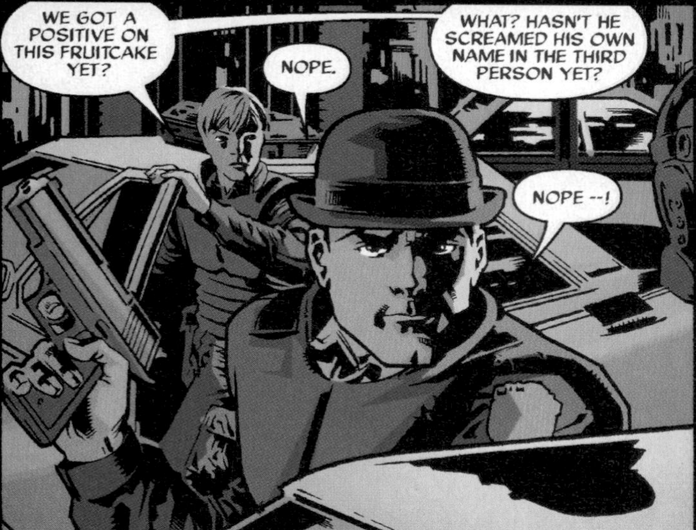
WE GOT A POSITIVE ON THIS FRUITCAKE YET?
NOPE.
WHAT? HASN'T HE SCREAMED HIS OWN NAME IN THE THIRD PERSON YET?
NOPE --!

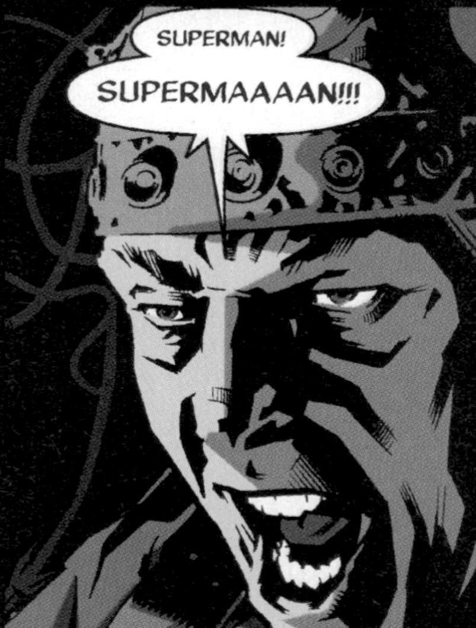
SUPERMAN!
SUPERMAAAAN!!!

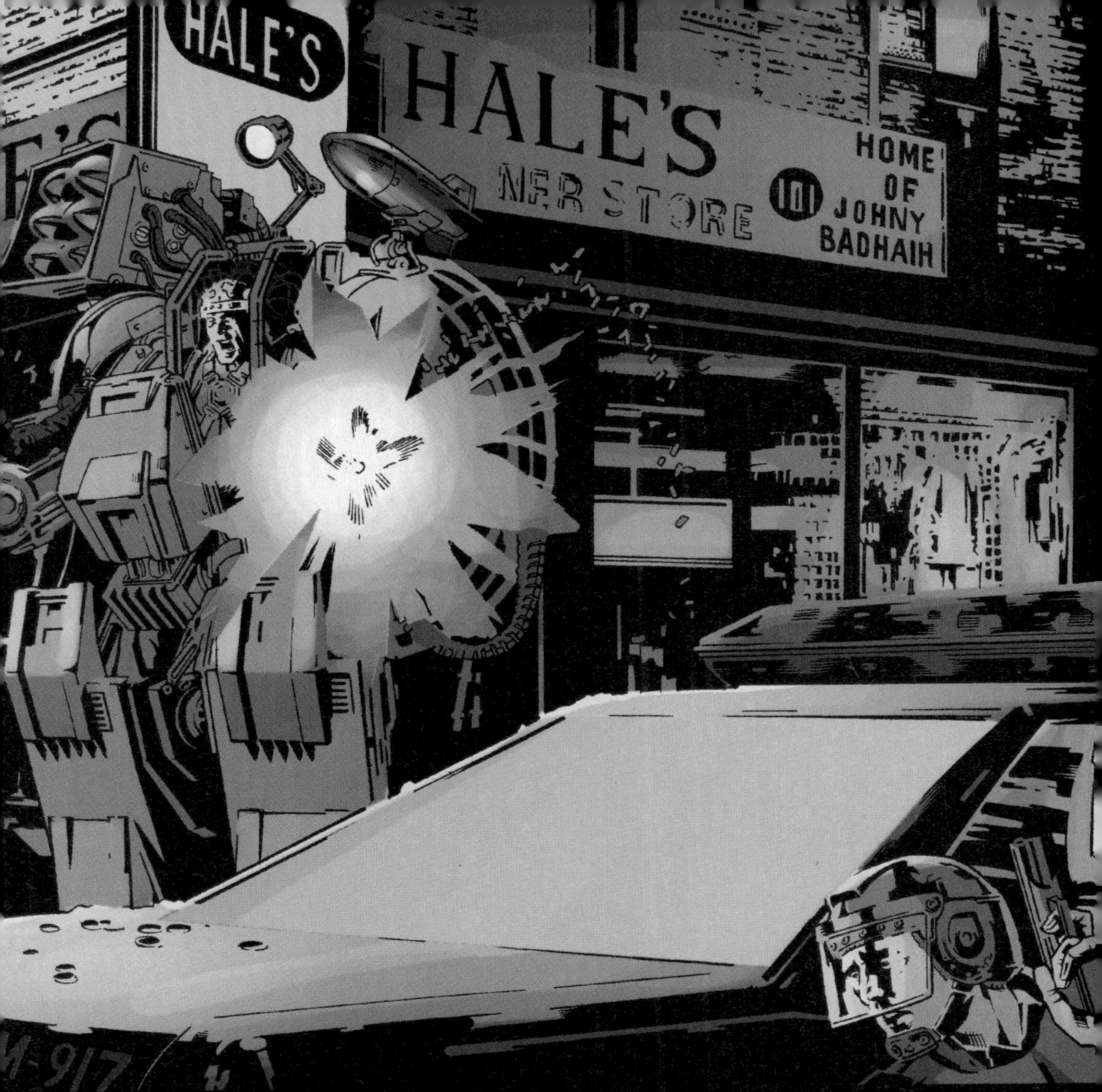
HALE'S
HALE'S
HOME OF JOHNY BADHAIH
M-917

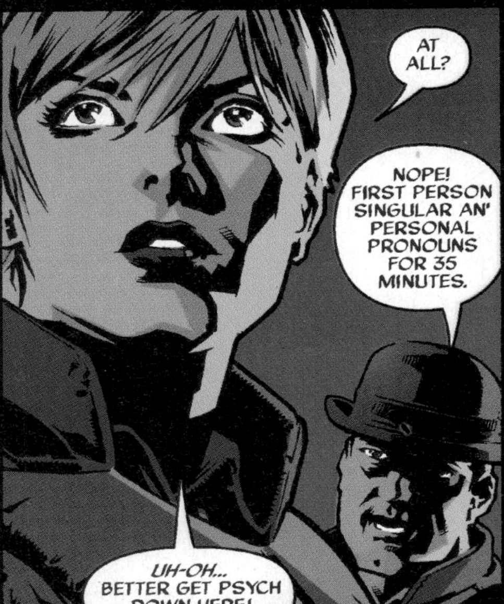
AT ALL?
NOPE! FIRST PERSON SINGULAR AN' PERSONAL PRONOUNS FOR 35 MINUTES.
UH-OH... BETTER GET PSYCH DOWN HERE!

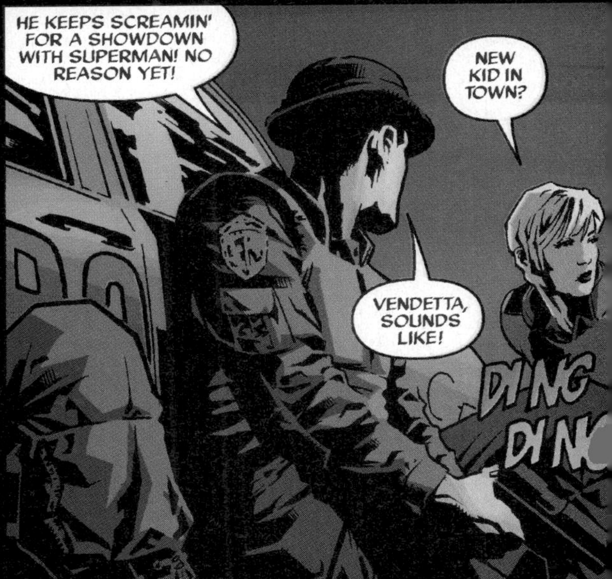
HE KEEPS SCREAMIN' FOR A SHOWDOWN WITH SUPERMAN! NO REASON YET!
NEW KID IN TOWN?
VENDETTA, SOUNDS LIKE!
DING
DING

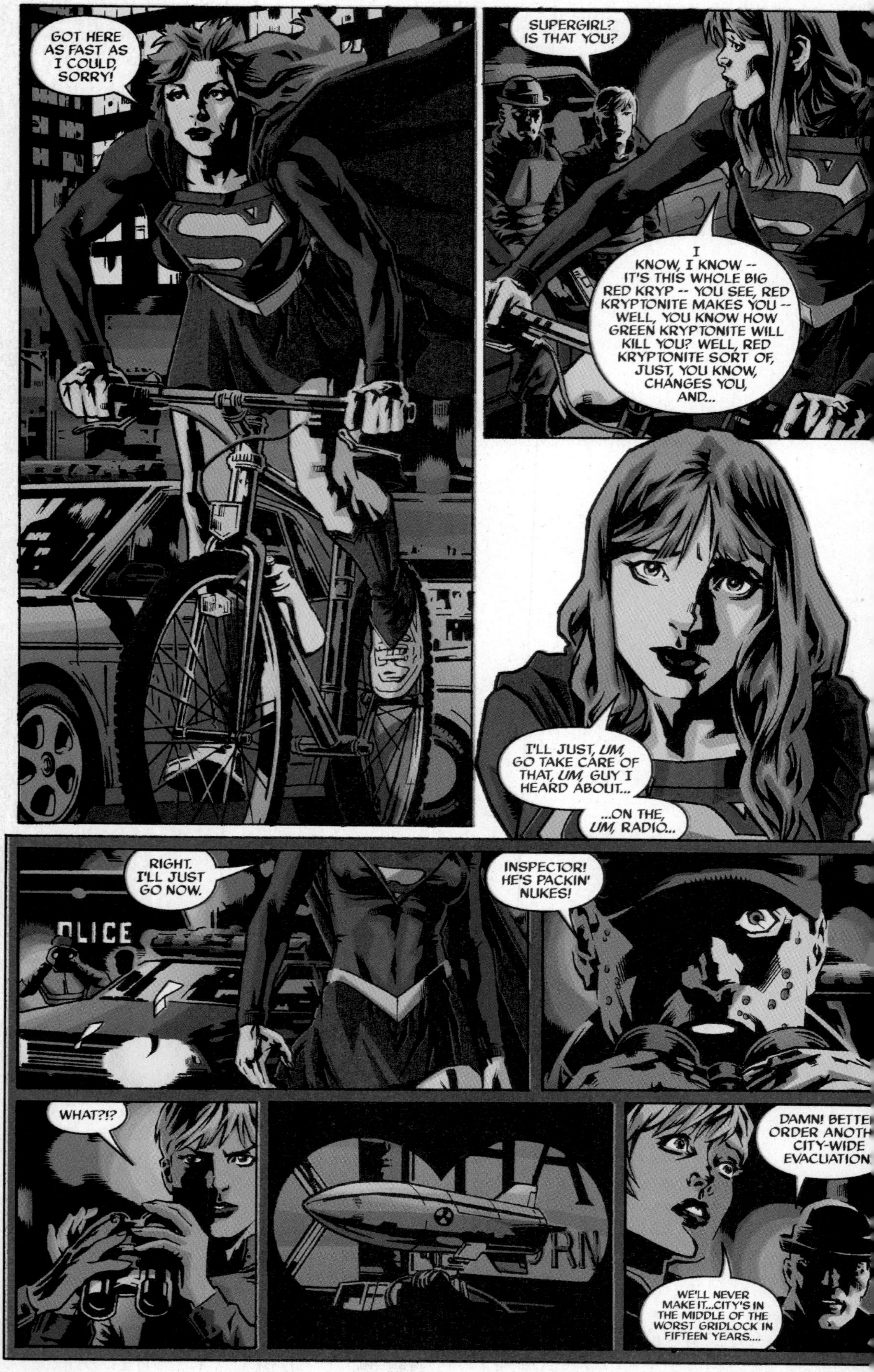
GOT HERE AS FAST AS I COULD, SORRY!
SUPERGIRL? IS THAT YOU?
I KNOW, I KNOW -- IT'S THIS WHOLE BIG RED KRYP -- YOU SEE, RED KRYPTONITE MAKES YOU -- WELL, YOU KNOW HOW GREEN KRYPTONITE WILL KILL YOU? WELL, RED KRYPTONITE SORT OF, JUST, YOU KNOW, CHANGES YOU, AND...
I'LL JUST, *UM*, GO TAKE CARE OF THAT, *UM*, GUY I HEARD ABOUT...
...ON THE, *UM*, RADIO...
RIGHT. I'LL JUST GO NOW.
OLICE
INSPECTOR! HE'S PACKIN' NUKES!
WHAT?!?
DAMN! BETTE ORDER ANOTH CITY-WIDE EVACUATION
WE'LL NEVER MAKE IT...CITY'S IN THE MIDDLE OF THE WORST GRIDLOCK IN FIFTEEN YEARS....

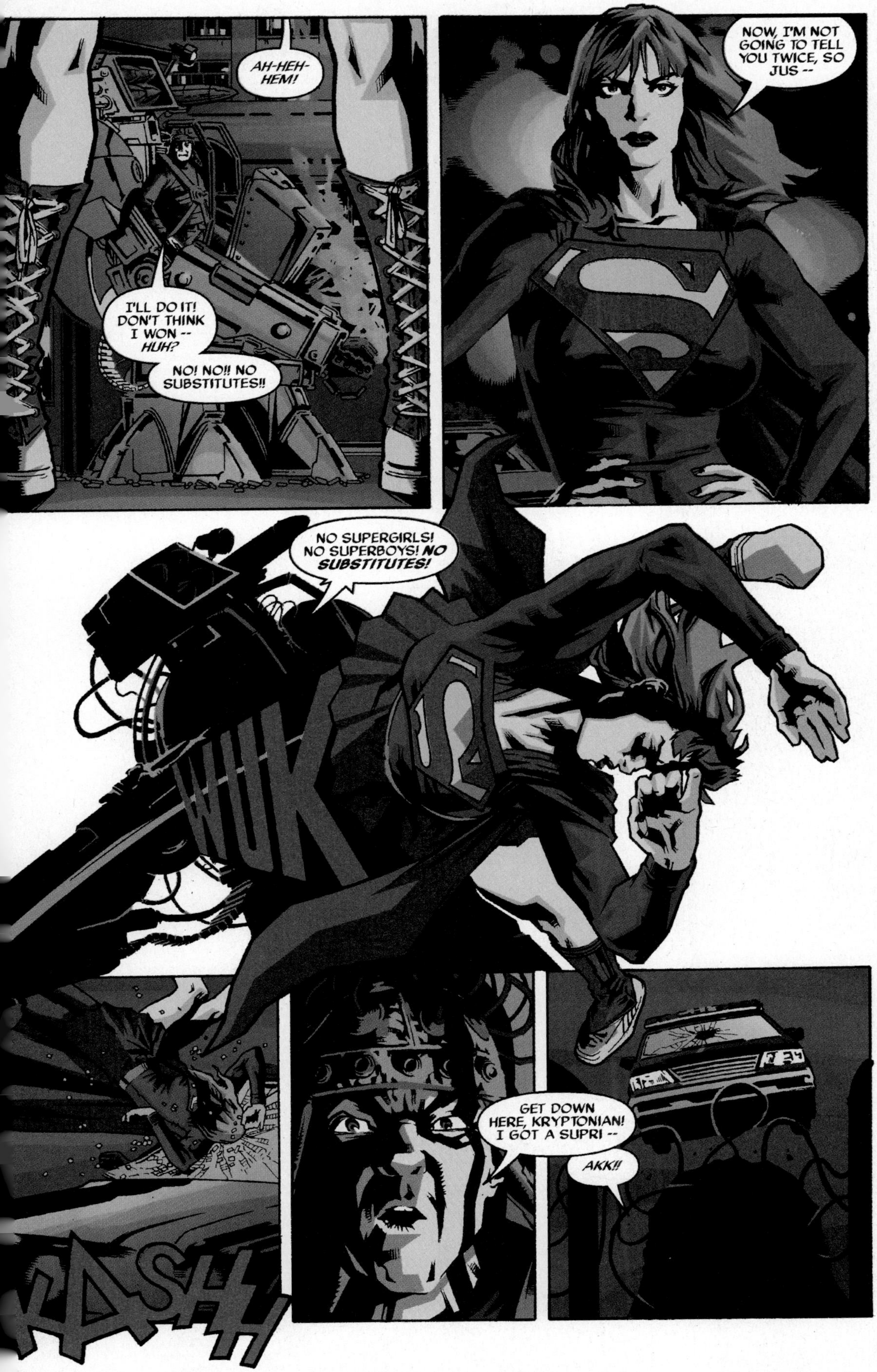
AH-HEH-HEM!
I'LL DO IT! DON'T THINK I WON -- HUH?
NO! NO!! NO SUBSTITUTES!!
NOW, I'M NOT GOING TO TELL YOU TWICE, SO JUS --
NO SUPERGIRLS! NO SUPERBOYS! NO SUBSTITUTES!
WUK
GET DOWN HERE, KRYPTONIAN! I GOT A SUPRI --
AKK!!

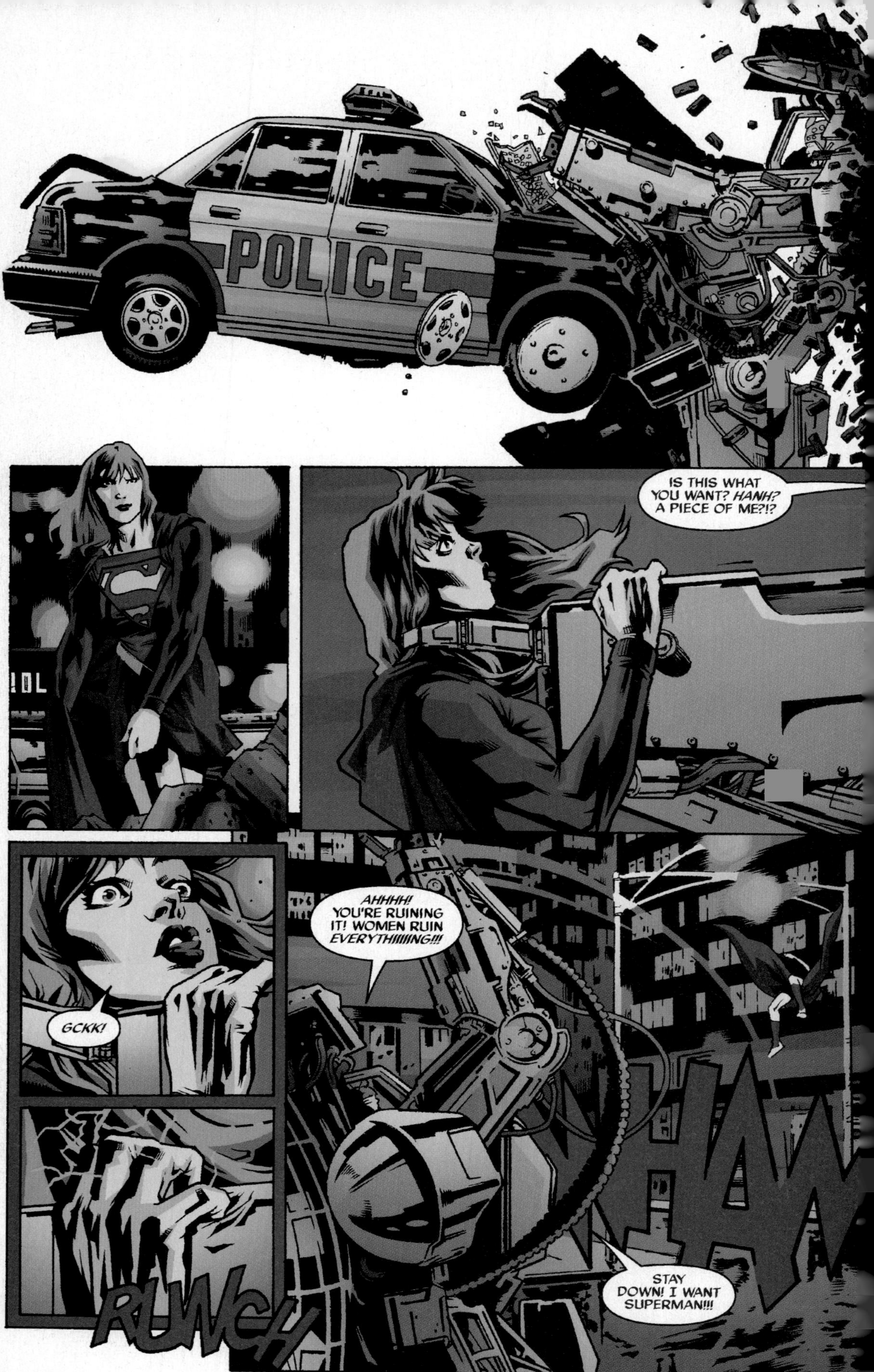
POLICE
IS THIS WHAT YOU WANT? HANH? A PIECE OF ME?!?
GCKK!
AHHHH! YOU'RE RUINING IT! WOMEN RUIN EVERYTHIIIIING!!!
STAY DOWN! I WANT SUPERMAN!!!
RUNCH

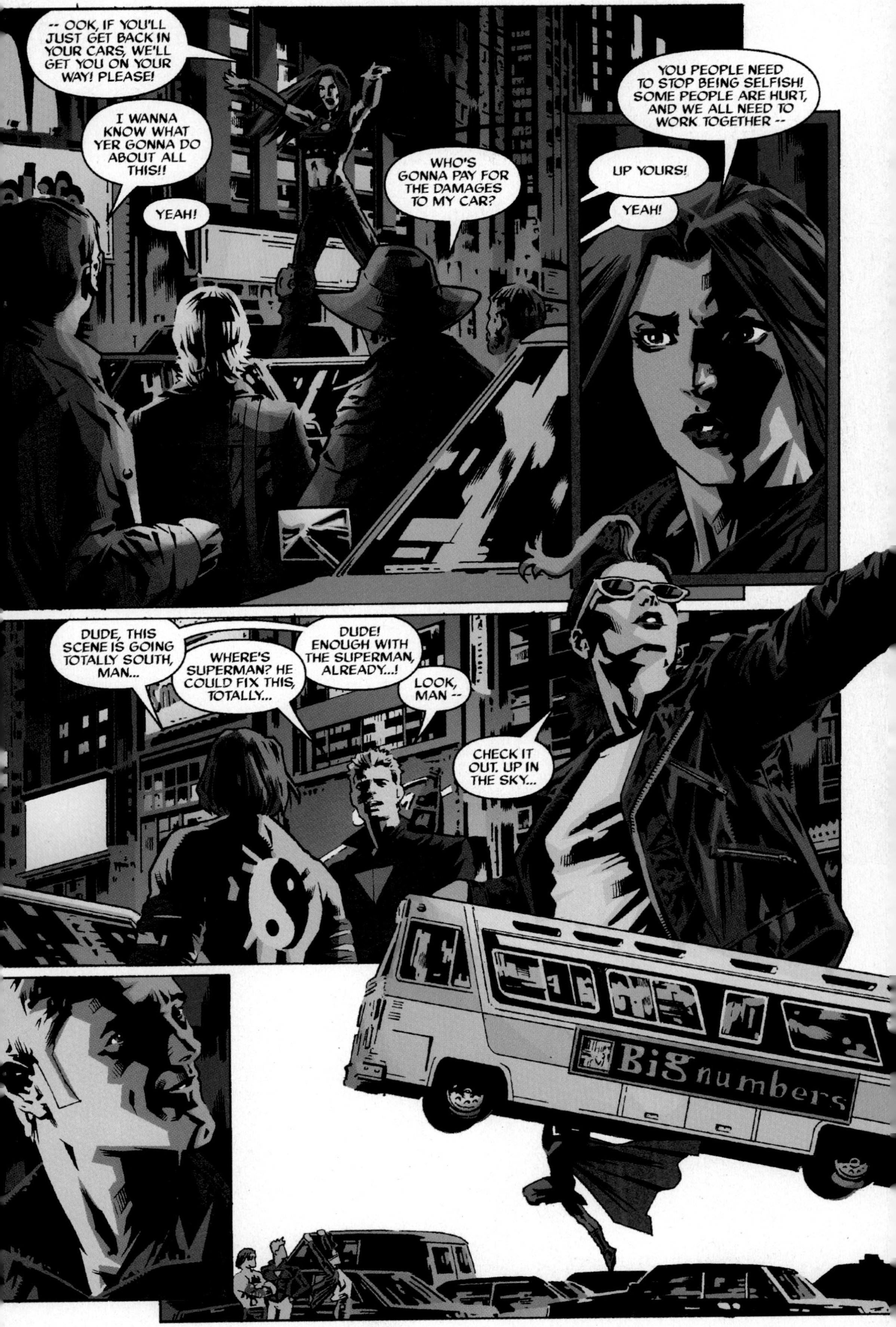
-- OOK, IF YOU'LL JUST GET BACK IN YOUR CARS, WE'LL GET YOU ON YOUR WAY! PLEASE!
I WANNA KNOW WHAT YER GONNA DO ABOUT ALL THIS!!
YEAH!
WHO'S GONNA PAY FOR THE DAMAGES TO MY CAR?
YOU PEOPLE NEED TO STOP BEING SELFISH! SOME PEOPLE ARE HURT, AND WE ALL NEED TO WORK TOGETHER --
UP YOURS!
YEAH!
DUDE, THIS SCENE IS GOING TOTALLY SOUTH, MAN...
WHERE'S SUPERMAN? HE COULD FIX THIS, TOTALLY...
DUDE! ENOUGH WITH THE SUPERMAN, ALREADY...!
LOOK, MAN --
CHECK IT OUT. UP IN THE SKY...
Big numbers

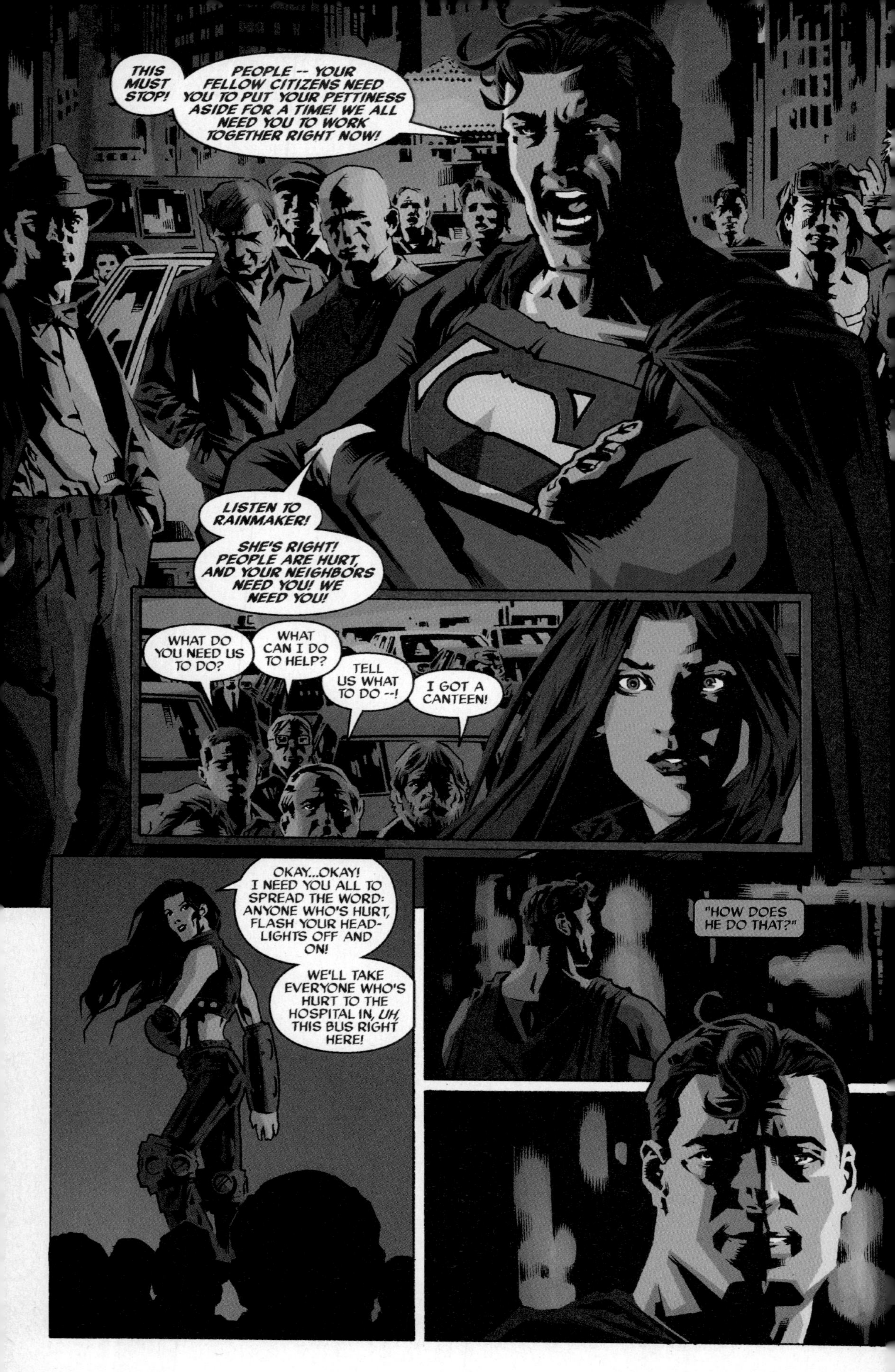
THIS MUST STOP!
PEOPLE -- YOUR FELLOW CITIZENS NEED YOU TO PUT YOUR PETTINESS ASIDE FOR A TIME! WE ALL NEED YOU TO WORK TOGETHER RIGHT NOW!
LISTEN TO RAINMAKER!
SHE'S RIGHT! PEOPLE ARE HURT, AND YOUR NEIGHBORS NEED YOU! WE NEED YOU!
WHAT DO YOU NEED US TO DO?
WHAT CAN I DO TO HELP?
TELL US WHAT TO DO --!
I GOT A CANTEEN!
OKAY...OKAY! I NEED YOU ALL TO SPREAD THE WORD: ANYONE WHO'S HURT, FLASH YOUR HEAD-LIGHTS OFF AND ON!
WE'LL TAKE EVERYONE WHO'S HURT TO THE HOSPITAL IN, UH, THIS BUS RIGHT HERE!
"HOW DOES HE DO THAT?"

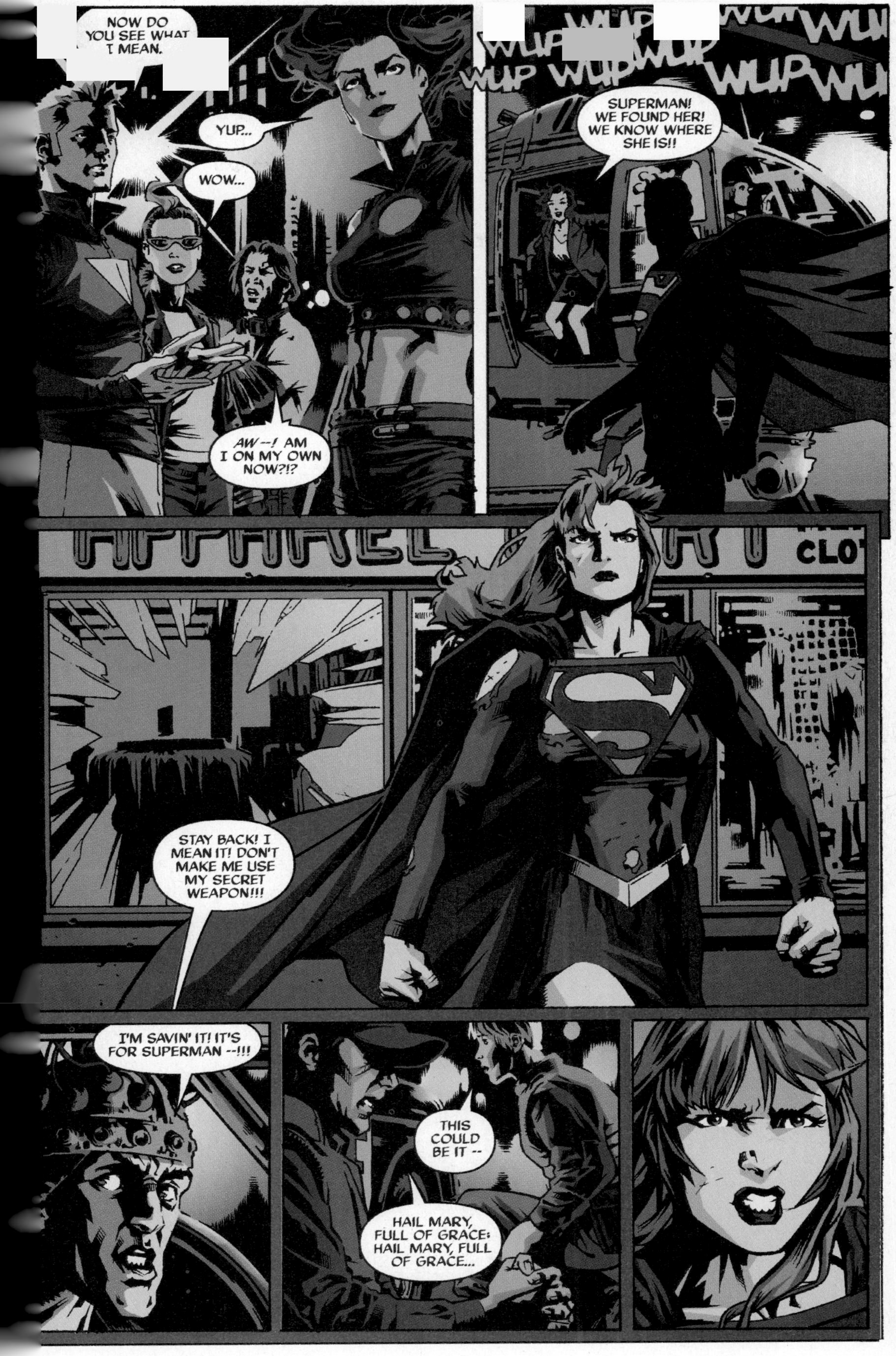
NOW DO YOU SEE WHAT I MEAN.
YUP...
WOW...
AW--! AM I ON MY OWN NOW?!?
SUPERMAN! WE FOUND HER! WE KNOW WHERE SHE IS!!
STAY BACK! I MEAN IT! DON'T MAKE ME USE MY SECRET WEAPON!!!
I'M SAVIN' IT! IT'S FOR SUPERMAN --!!!
THIS COULD BE IT --
HAIL MARY, FULL OF GRACE: HAIL MARY, FULL OF GRACE...

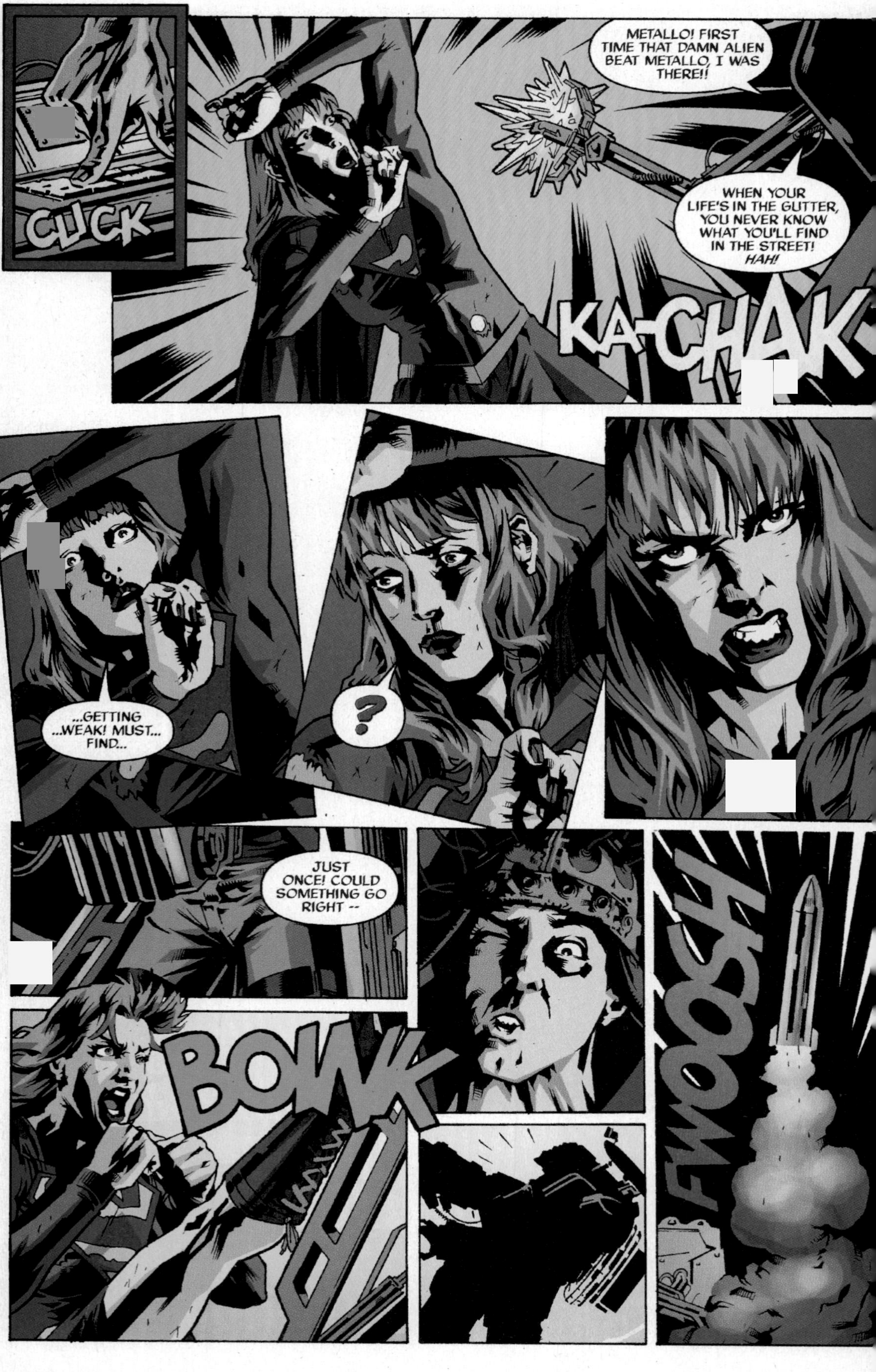
CLICK
METALLO! FIRST TIME THAT DAMN ALIEN BEAT METALLO, I WAS THERE!!
WHEN YOUR LIFE'S IN THE GUTTER, YOU NEVER KNOW WHAT YOU'LL FIND IN THE STREET! *HAH!*
KA-CHAK
...GETTING ...WEAK! MUST... FIND...
?
JUST ONCE! COULD SOMETHING GO RIGHT --
BONK
FWOOSH

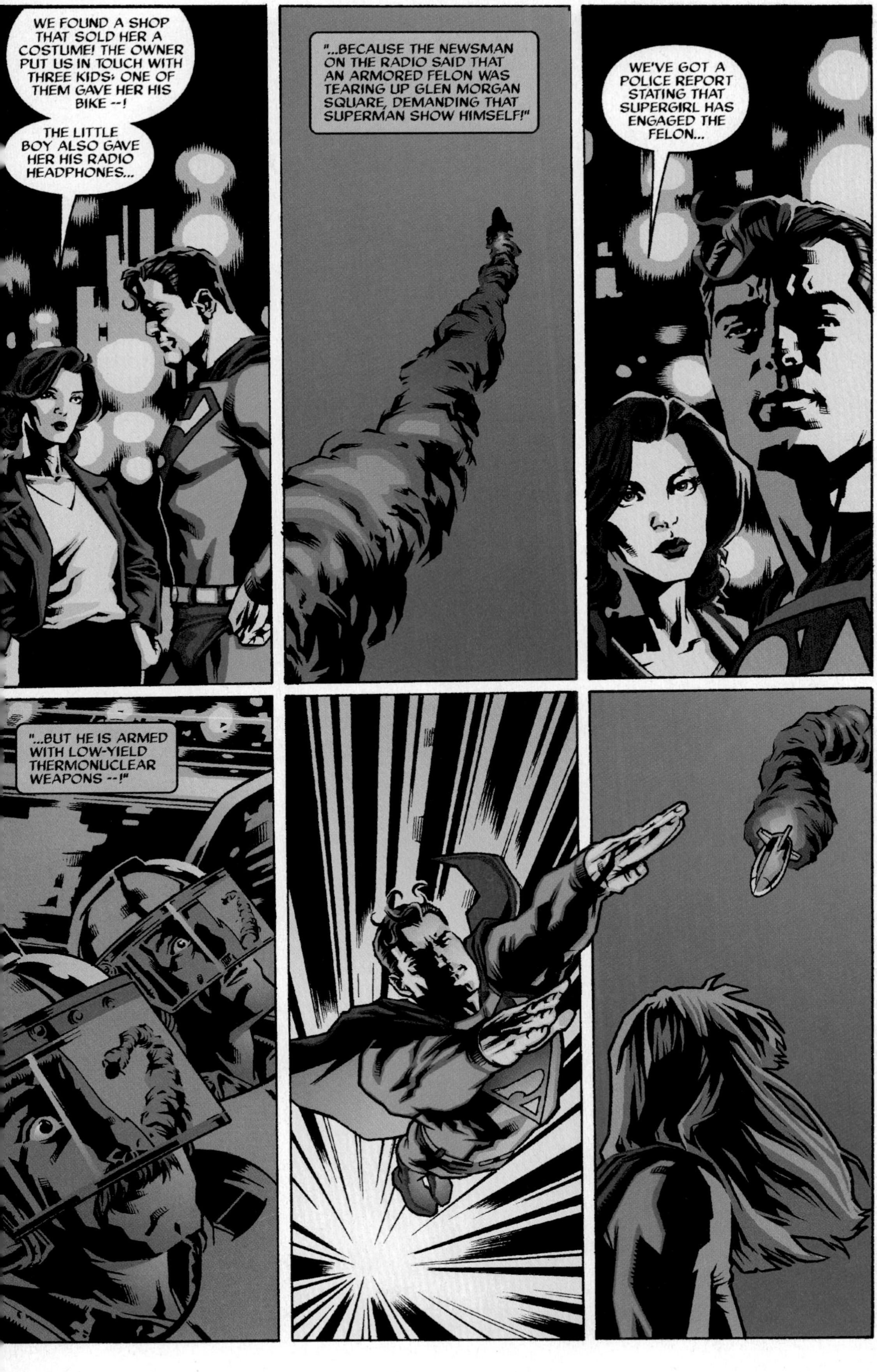
WE FOUND A SHOP THAT SOLD HER A COSTUME! THE OWNER PUT US IN TOUCH WITH THREE KIDS; ONE OF THEM GAVE HER HIS BIKE --!
THE LITTLE BOY ALSO GAVE HER HIS RADIO HEADPHONES...
"...BECAUSE THE NEWSMAN ON THE RADIO SAID THAT AN ARMORED FELON WAS TEARING UP GLEN MORGAN SQUARE, DEMANDING THAT SUPERMAN SHOW HIMSELF!"
WE'VE GOT A POLICE REPORT STATING THAT SUPERGIRL HAS ENGAGED THE FELON...
"...BUT HE IS ARMED WITH LOW-YIELD THERMONUCLEAR WEAPONS --!"

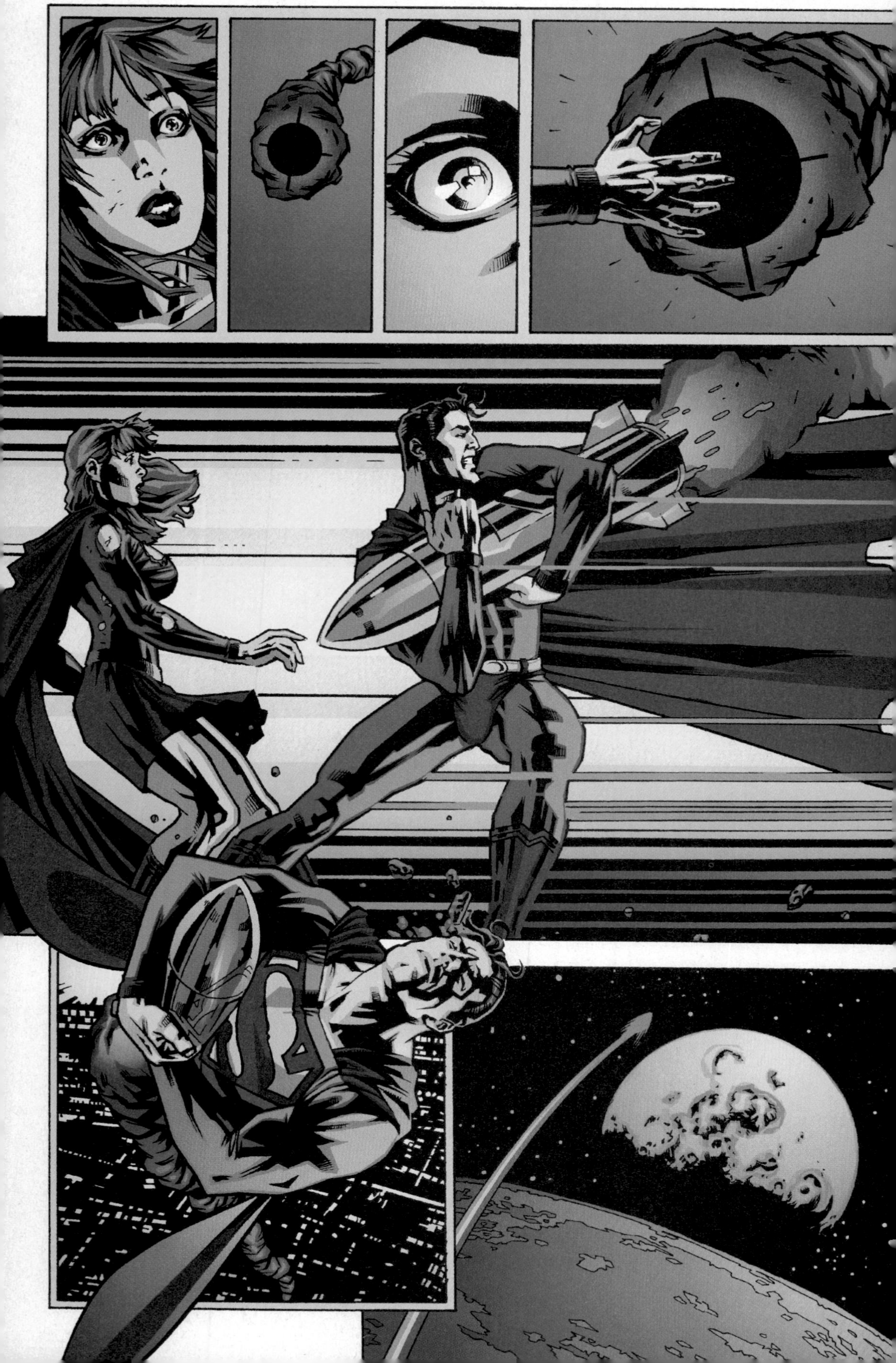

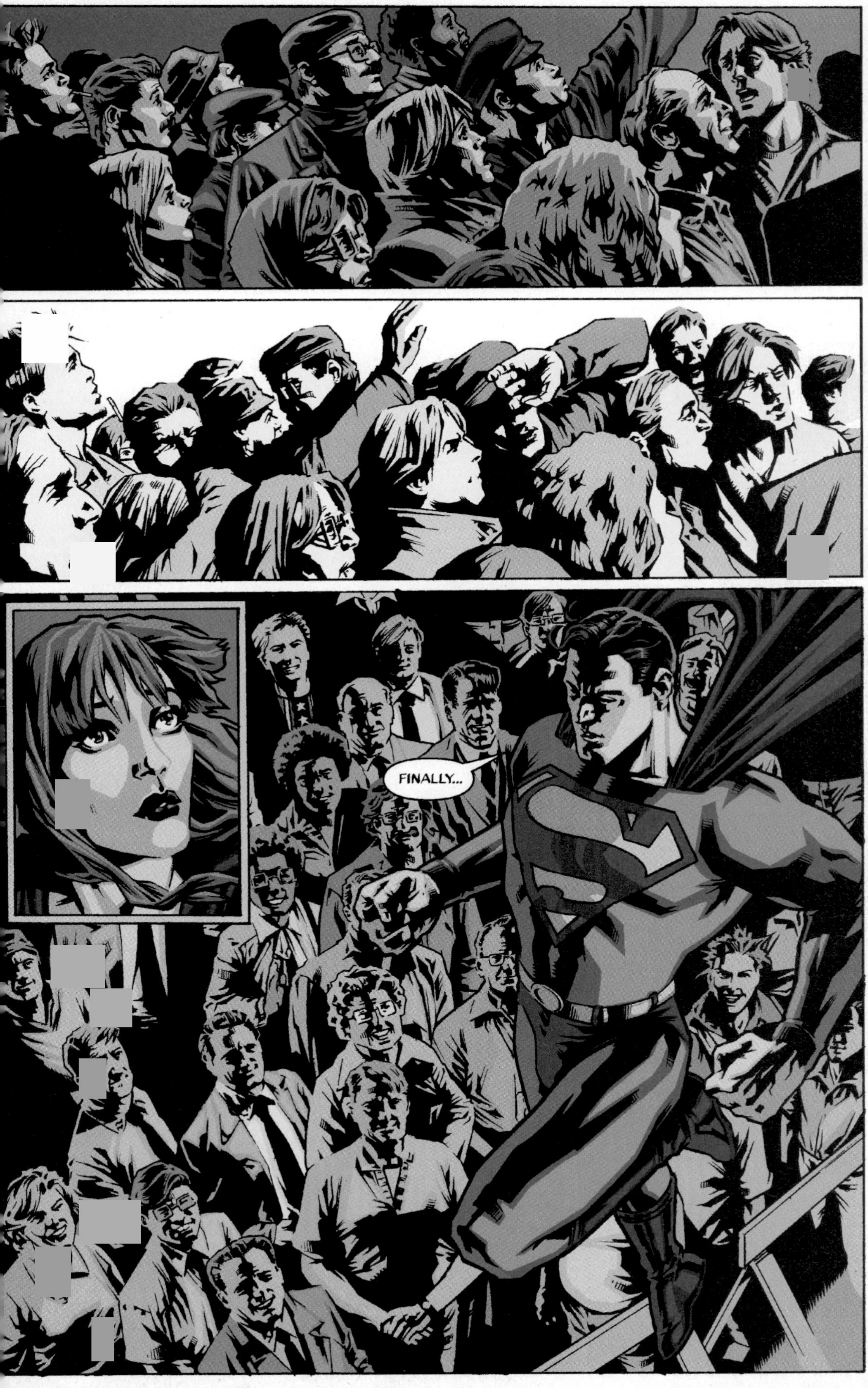
FINALLY...

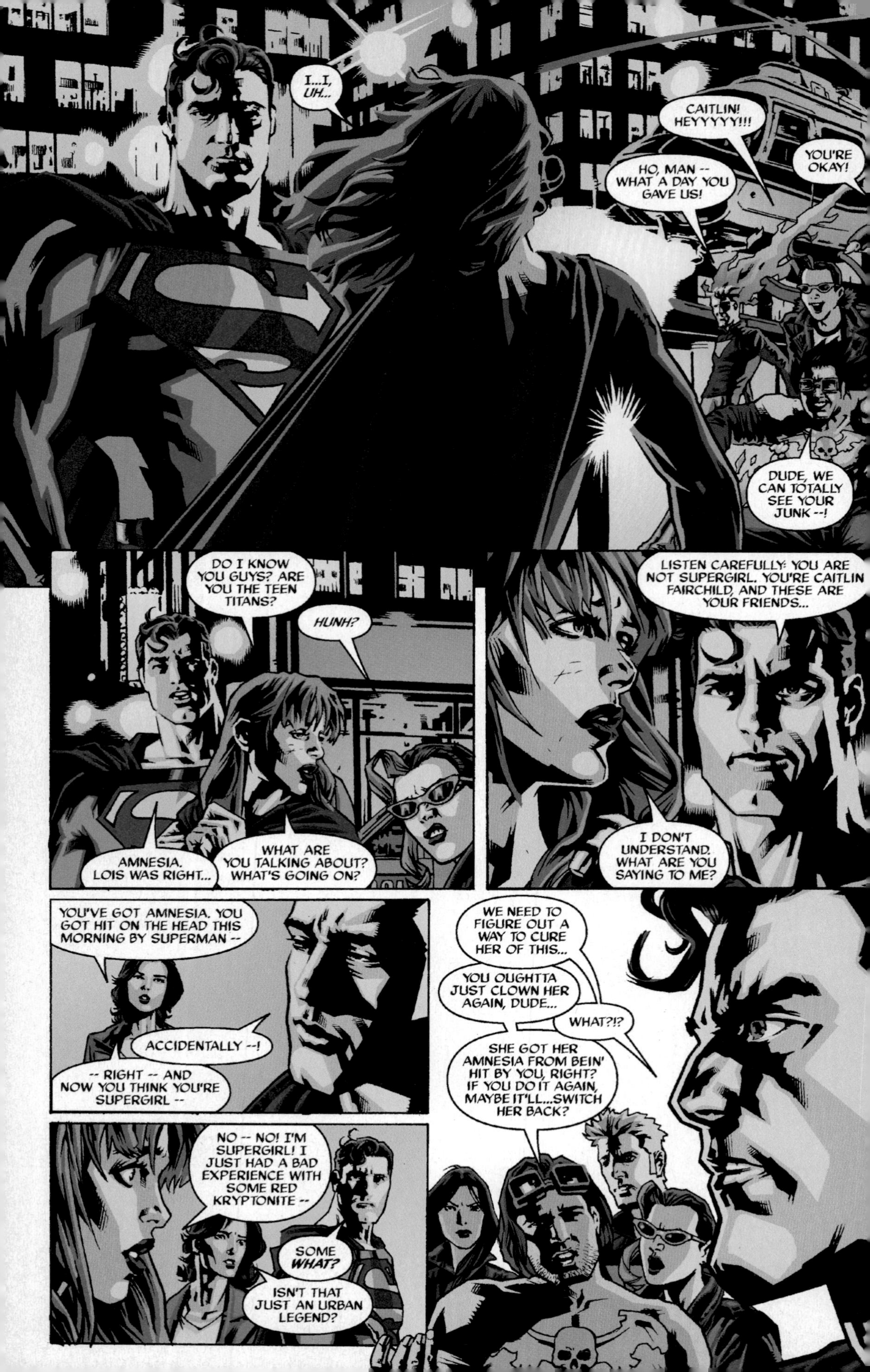
I...I, UH...
CAITLIN! HEYYYYY!!!
HO, MAN -- WHAT A DAY YOU GAVE US!
YOU'RE OKAY!
DUDE, WE CAN TOTALLY SEE YOUR JUNK --!
DO I KNOW YOU GUYS? ARE YOU THE TEEN TITANS?
HUNH?
AMNESIA. LOIS WAS RIGHT...
WHAT ARE YOU TALKING ABOUT? WHAT'S GOING ON?
LISTEN CAREFULLY: YOU ARE NOT SUPERGIRL. YOU'RE CAITLIN FAIRCHILD, AND THESE ARE YOUR FRIENDS...
I DON'T UNDERSTAND. WHAT ARE YOU SAYING TO ME?
YOU'VE GOT AMNESIA. YOU GOT HIT ON THE HEAD THIS MORNING BY SUPERMAN --
ACCIDENTALLY --!
-- RIGHT -- AND NOW YOU THINK YOU'RE SUPERGIRL --
WE NEED TO FIGURE OUT A WAY TO CURE HER OF THIS...
YOU OUGHTTA JUST CLOWN HER AGAIN, DUDE...
WHAT?!?
SHE GOT HER AMNESIA FROM BEIN' HIT BY YOU, RIGHT? IF YOU DO IT AGAIN, MAYBE IT'LL...SWITCH HER BACK?
NO -- NO! I'M SUPERGIRL! I JUST HAD A BAD EXPERIENCE WITH SOME RED KRYPTONITE --
SOME WHAT?
ISN'T THAT JUST AN URBAN LEGEND?

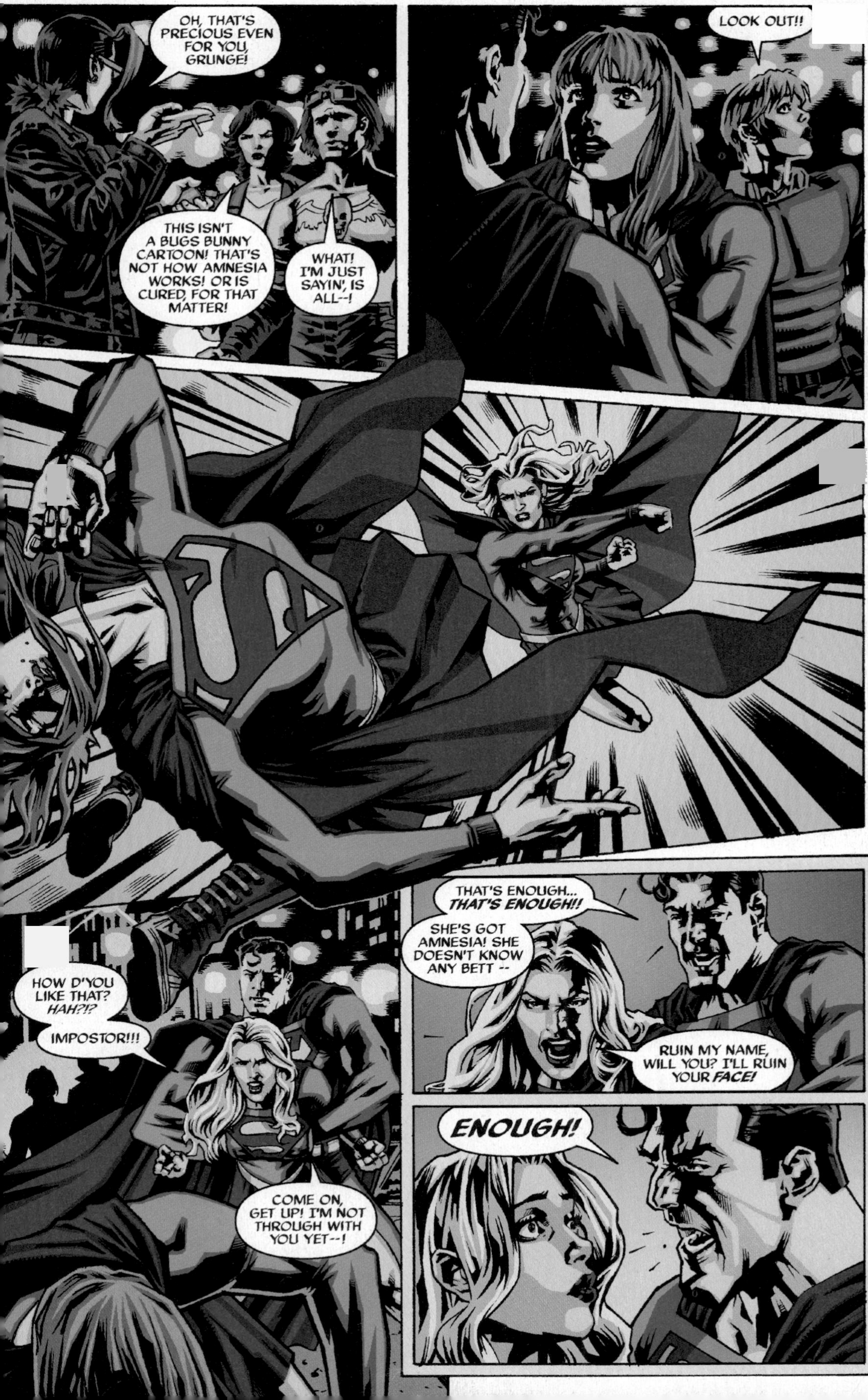
OH, THAT'S PRECIOUS EVEN FOR YOU, GRUNGE!
THIS ISN'T A BUGS BUNNY CARTOON! THAT'S NOT HOW AMNESIA WORKS! OR IS CURED, FOR THAT MATTER!
WHAT! I'M JUST SAYIN', IS ALL--!
LOOK OUT!!
HOW D'YOU LIKE THAT? *HAH?!?*
IMPOSTOR!!!
COME ON, GET UP! I'M NOT THROUGH WITH YOU YET--!
THAT'S ENOUGH... *THAT'S ENOUGH!!*
SHE'S GOT AMNESIA! SHE DOESN'T KNOW ANY BETT --
RUIN MY NAME, WILL YOU? I'LL RUIN YOUR *FACE!*
ENOUGH!

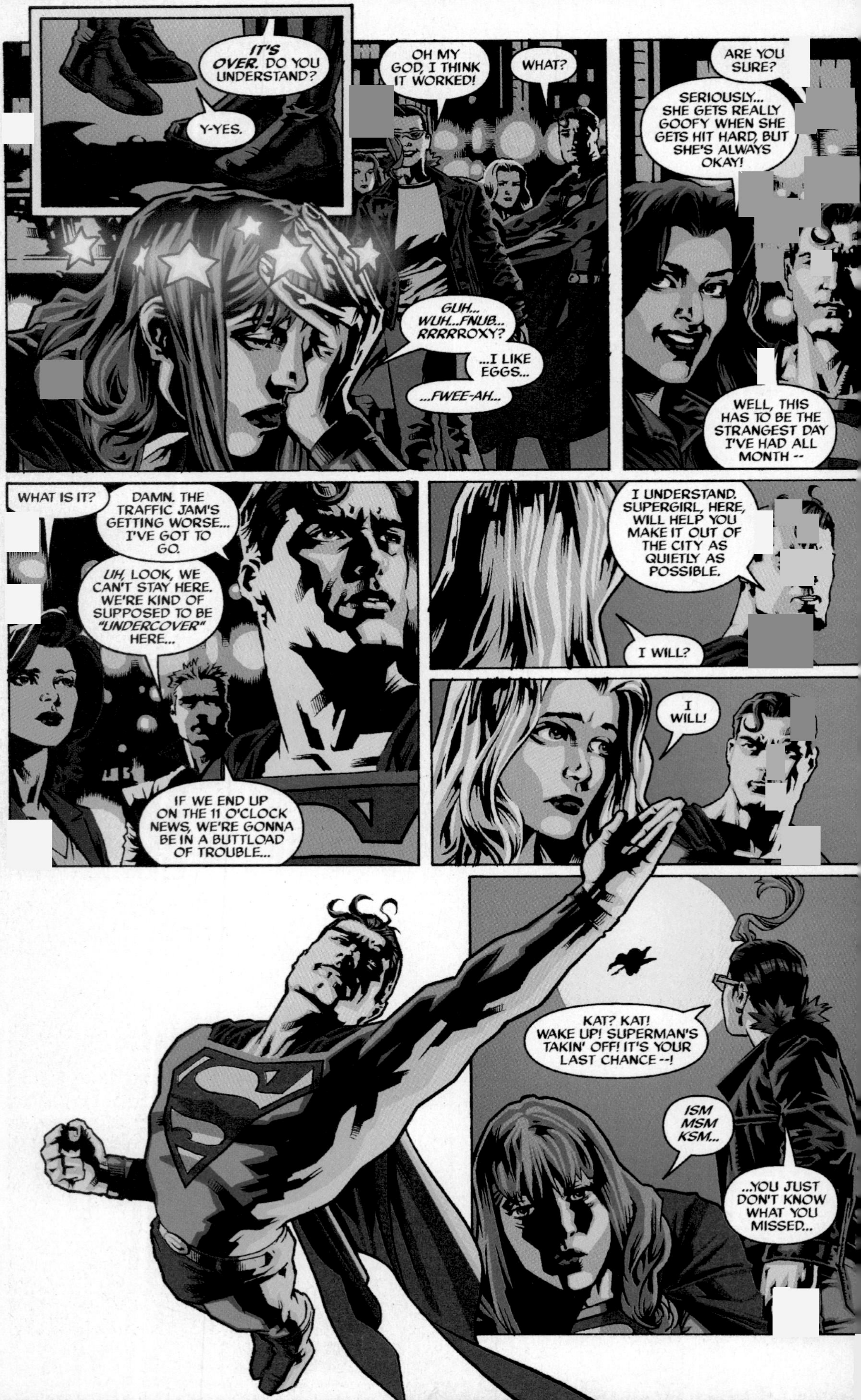
IT'S OVER. DO YOU UNDERSTAND?
Y-YES.
OH MY GOD, I THINK IT WORKED!
WHAT?
ARE YOU SURE?
SERIOUSLY... SHE GETS REALLY GOOFY WHEN SHE GETS HIT HARD, BUT SHE'S ALWAYS OKAY!
GUH... WUH...FNUB... RRRRROXY?
...I LIKE EGGS...
...FWEE-AH...
WELL, THIS HAS TO BE THE STRANGEST DAY I'VE HAD ALL MONTH --
WHAT IS IT?
DAMN. THE TRAFFIC JAM'S GETTING WORSE... I'VE GOT TO GO.
UH, LOOK, WE CAN'T STAY HERE. WE'RE KIND OF SUPPOSED TO BE "UNDERCOVER" HERE...
IF WE END UP ON THE 11 O'CLOCK NEWS, WE'RE GONNA BE IN A BUTTLOAD OF TROUBLE...
I UNDERSTAND. SUPERGIRL, HERE, WILL HELP YOU MAKE IT OUT OF THE CITY AS QUIETLY AS POSSIBLE.
I WILL?
I WILL!
KAT? KAT! WAKE UP! SUPERMAN'S TAKIN' OFF! IT'S YOUR LAST CHANCE --!
ISM MSM KSM...
...YOU JUST DON'T KNOW WHAT YOU MISSED...

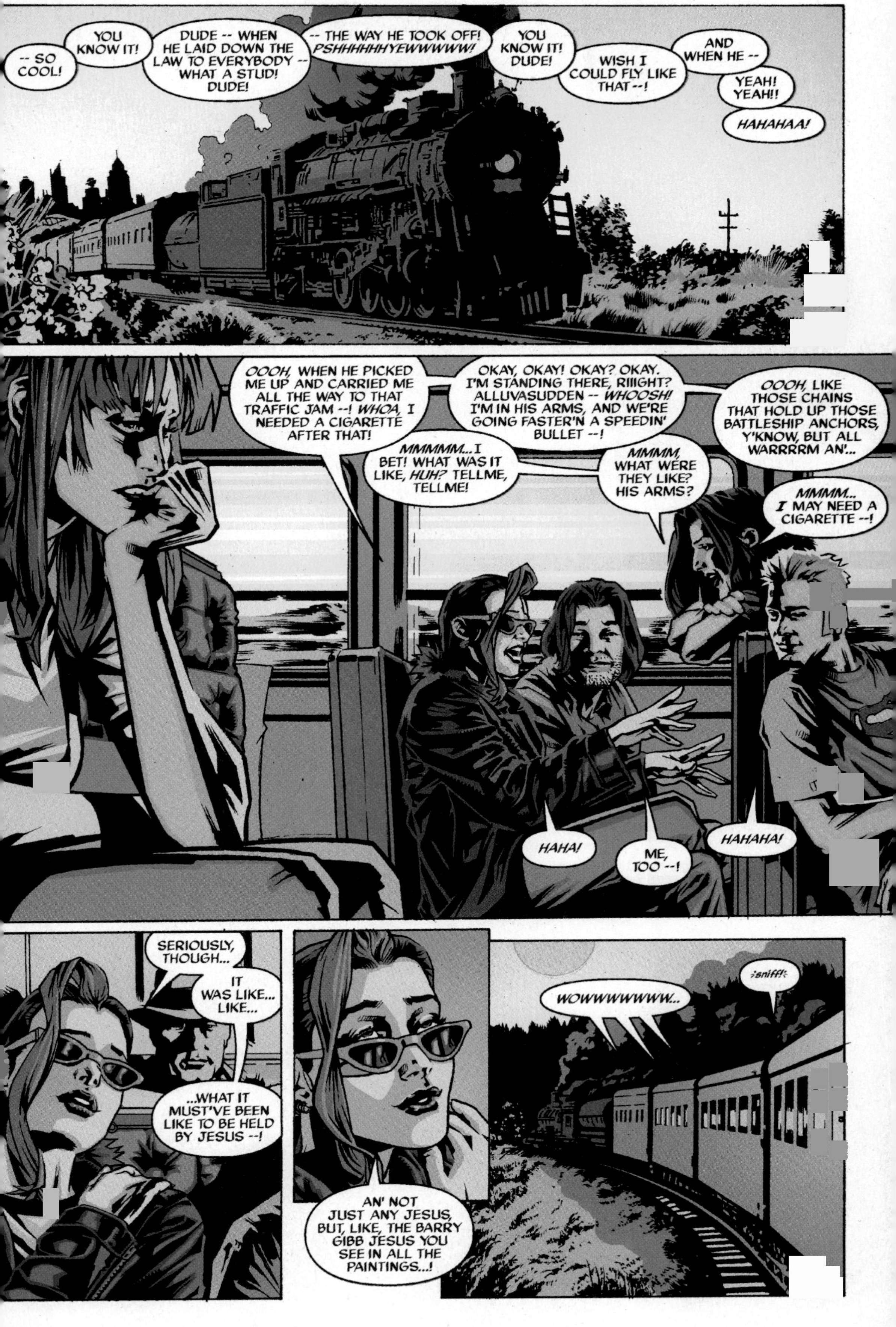
-- SO COOL!
YOU KNOW IT!
DUDE -- WHEN HE LAID DOWN THE LAW TO EVERYBODY -- WHAT A STUD! DUDE!
-- THE WAY HE TOOK OFF! PSHHHHHHYEWWWWW!
YOU KNOW IT! DUDE!
WISH I COULD FLY LIKE THAT --!
AND WHEN HE --
YEAH! YEAH!!
HAHAHAA!
OOOH, WHEN HE PICKED ME UP AND CARRIED ME ALL THE WAY TO THAT TRAFFIC JAM --! WHOA, I NEEDED A CIGARETTE AFTER THAT!
OKAY, OKAY! OKAY? OKAY. I'M STANDING THERE, RIIIGHT? ALLUVASUDDEN -- WHOOSH! I'M IN HIS ARMS, AND WE'RE GOING FASTER'N A SPEEDIN' BULLET --!
OOOH, LIKE THOSE CHAINS THAT HOLD UP THOSE BATTLESHIP ANCHORS, Y'KNOW, BUT ALL WARRRRM AN'...
MMMMM... I BET! WHAT WAS IT LIKE, HUH? TELLME, TELLME!
MMMM, WHAT WERE THEY LIKE? HIS ARMS?
MMMM... I MAY NEED A CIGARETTE --!
HAHA!
ME, TOO --!
HAHAHA!
SERIOUSLY, THOUGH...
IT WAS LIKE... LIKE...
...WHAT IT MUST'VE BEEN LIKE TO BE HELD BY JESUS --!
AN' NOT JUST ANY JESUS, BUT, LIKE, THE BARRY GIBB JESUS YOU SEE IN ALL THE PAINTINGS...!
WOWWWWWWW...
;sniff!;

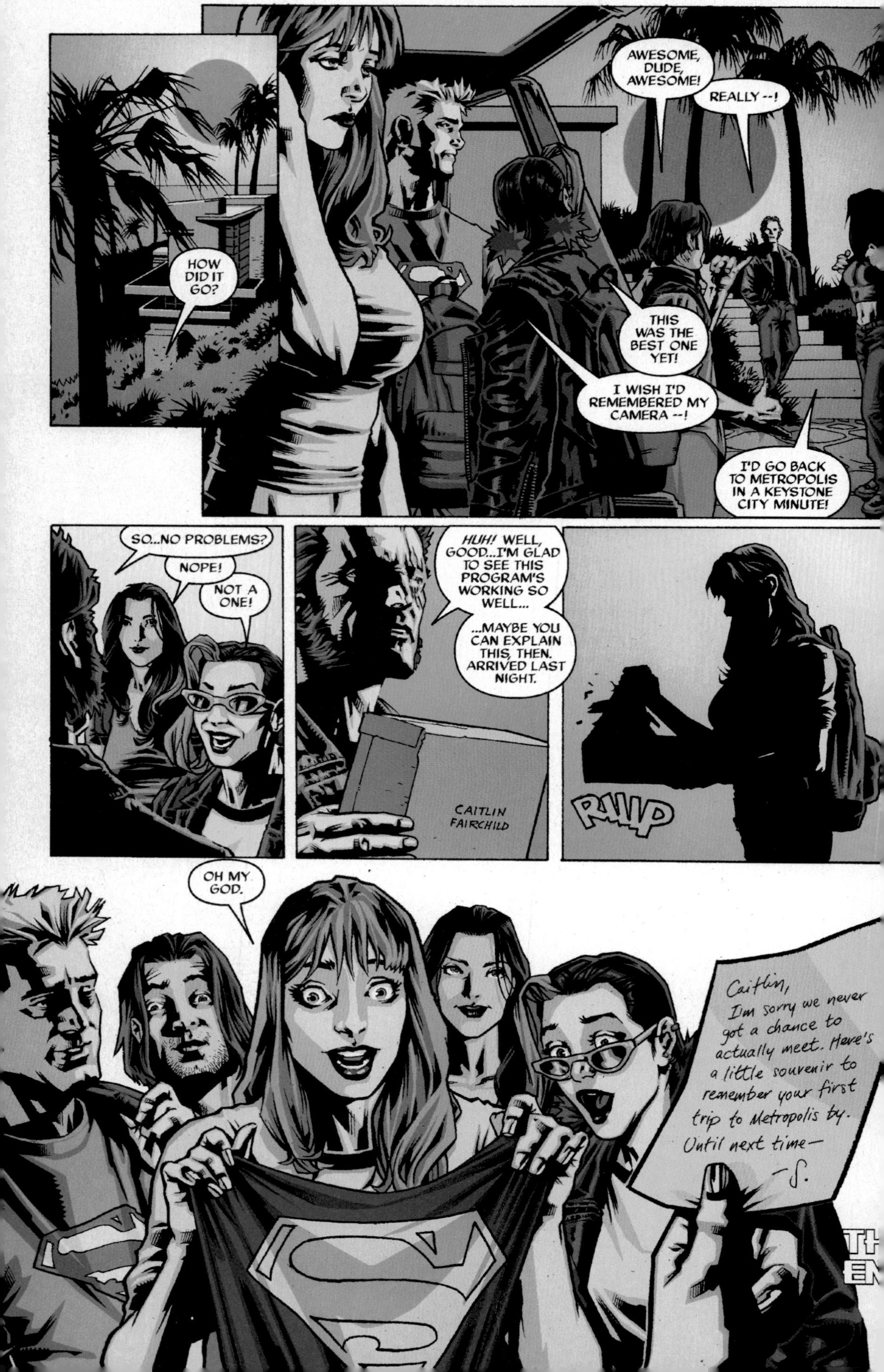
HOW DID IT GO?
AWESOME, DUDE, AWESOME!
REALLY --!
THIS WAS THE BEST ONE YET!
I WISH I'D REMEMBERED MY CAMERA --!
I'D GO BACK TO METROPOLIS IN A KEYSTONE CITY MINUTE!
SO...NO PROBLEMS?
NOPE!
NOT A ONE!
HUH! WELL, GOOD...I'M GLAD TO SEE THIS PROGRAM'S WORKING SO WELL...
...MAYBE YOU CAN EXPLAIN THIS, THEN. ARRIVED LAST NIGHT.
CAITLIN FAIRCHILD
RIIIP
OH MY GOD.
Caitlin,
I'm sorry we never got a chance to actually meet. Here's a little souvenir to remember your first trip to Metropolis by.
Until next time—
—S.

ALTERNATE COVER GALLERY

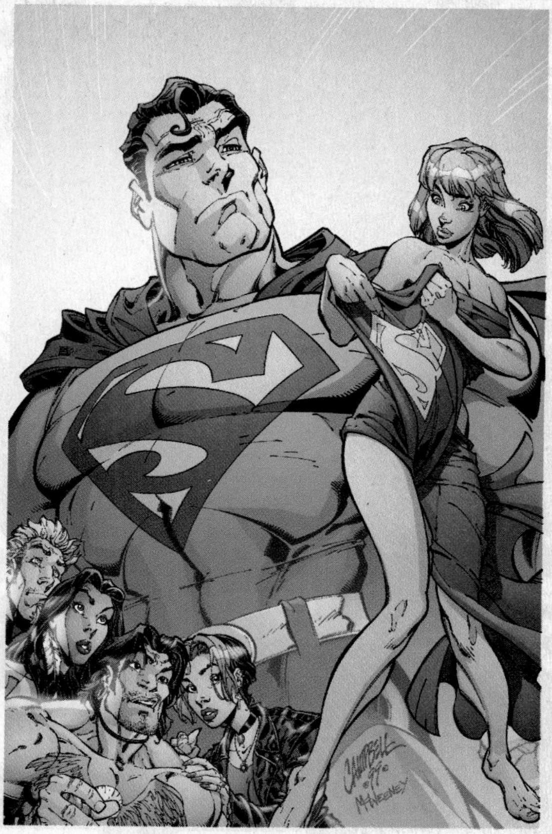

Superman/Gen[13] *#1 cover by J. Scott Campbell, Tom McWeeney & Guy Major*

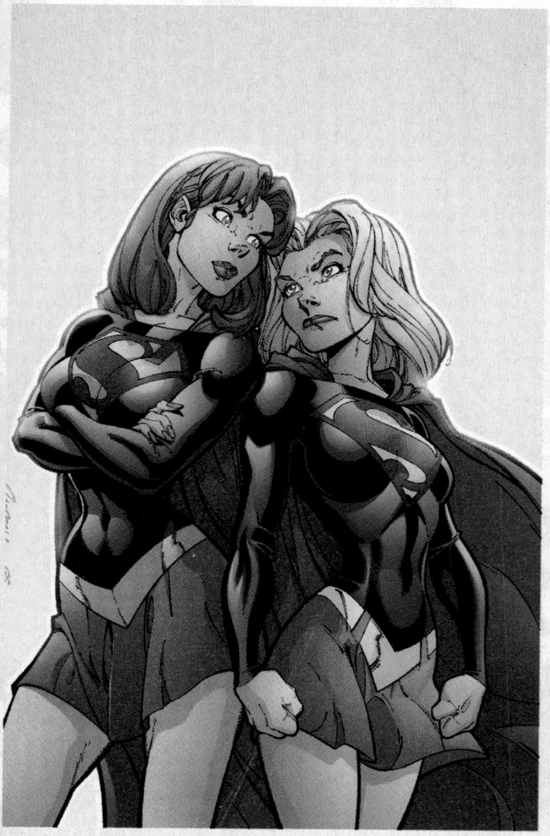

Superman/Gen[13] *#2 cover by J. Scott Campbell, Tom McWeeney & Guy Major*

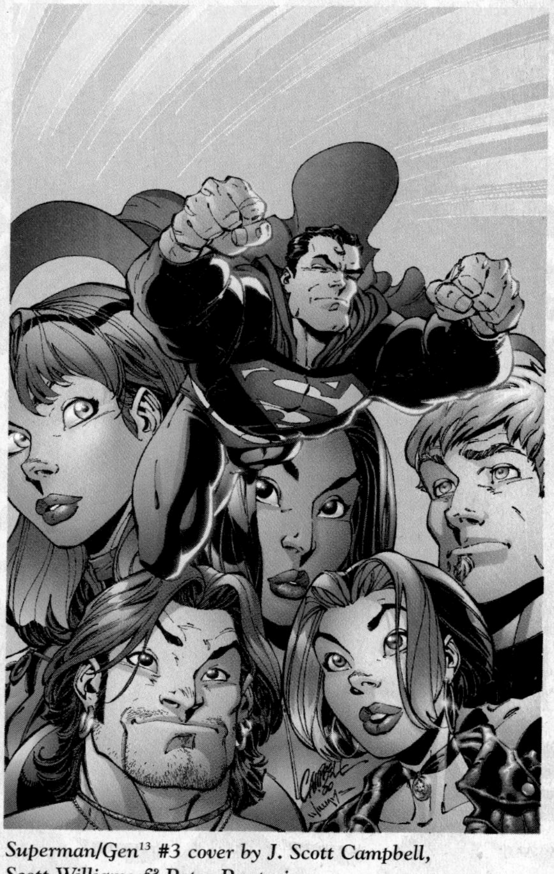

Superman/Gen[13] *#3 cover by J. Scott Campbell, Scott Williams & Peter Pantazis*

WILDSTORM COLLECTIONS

THE AUTHORITY: RELENTLESS
ELLIS/HITCH/NEARY

THE AUTHORITY:
UNDER NEW MANAGEMENT
ELLIS/MILLAR/HITCH/
QUITELY/NEARY/SCOTT

CRIMSON: LOYALTY & LOSS
AUGUSTYN/RAMOS/HOPE

CRIMSON:
HEAVEN & EARTH
AUGUSTYN/RAMOS/HOPE

CRIMSON:
EARTH ANGEL
AUGUSTYN/RAMOS/HOPE

DEATHBLOW:
SINNERS AND SAINTS
CHOI/LEE/SALE/SCOTT

DANGER GIRL:
THE DANGEROUS
COLLECTION #1-3
HARTNELL/CAMPBELL/GARNER

DIVINE RIGHT:
COLLECTED EDITION #1-3
LEE/WILLIAMS

GEN^{13}
CHOI/LEE/CAMPBELL/GARNER

GEN^{13}: #13 ABC
CHOI/LEE/CAMPBELL/GARNER

GEN^{13}: BOOTLEG VOL. 1
VARIOUS WRITERS AND
ARTISTS

GEN^{13}: GRUNGE THE MOVIE
WARREN

GEN^{13}: I LOVE NEW YORK
ARCUDI/FRANK/SMITH

GEN^{13}: INTERACTIVE PLUS
VARIOUS WRITERS AND
ARTISTS

GEN^{13}: STARTING OVER
CHOI/LEE/CAMPBELL/GARNER

GEN^{13}:
WE'LL TAKE MANHATTAN
LOBDELL/BENES/SIBAL

KURT BUSIEK'S ASTRO CITY:
LIFE IN THE BIG CITY
BUSIEK/ANDERSON

KURT BUSIEK'S ASTRO CITY:
CONFESSION
BUSIEK/ANDERSON/BLYBERG

KURT BUSIEK'S ASTRO CITY:
FAMILY ALBUM
BUSIEK/ANDERSON/BLYBERG

KURT BUSIEK'S ASTRO CITY:
TARNISHED ANGEL
BUSIEK/ANDERSON/BLYBERG

LEAVE IT TO CHANCE:
SHAMAN'S RAIN
ROBINSON/SMITH

LEAVE IT TO CHANCE:
TRICK OR THREAT
ROBINSON/SMITH/FREEMAN

WETWORKS: REBIRTH
PORTACIO/CHOI/WILLIAMS

PLANETARY/AUTHORITY:
RULING THE WORLD
ELLIS/JIMENEZ/LANNING

PLANETARY:
ALL OVER THE WORLD
AND OTHER STORIES
ELLIS/CASSADAY

PLANETARY:
THE FOURTH MAN
ELLIS/CASSADAY

STORMWATCH:
FORCE OF NATURE
ELLIS/RANEY/ELLIOTT

STORMWATCH:
LIGHTNING STRIKES
ELLIS/RANEY/LEE/
ELLIOTT/WILLIAMS

STORMWATCH:
CHANGE OR DIE
ELLIS/RANEY/JIMENEZ

STORMWATCH:
A FINER WORLD
ELLIS/HITCH/NEARY

WILDC.A.T.S: GANG WAR
MOORE/VARIOUS

WILDC.A.T.S:
GATHERING OF EAGLES
CLAREMONT/LEE/WILLIAMS

WILDC.A.T.S:
HOMECOMING
MOORE/VARIOUS

WILDC.A.T.S/X-MEN
VARIOUS WRITERS AND
ARTISTS

WILDCATS:
STREET SMART
LOBDELL/CHAREST/FRIEND

WILDCATS:
VICIOUS CIRCLES
CASEY/PHILLIPS

WILDSTORM RISING
WINDSOR-SMITH/VARIOUS

OTHER COLLECTIONS OF INTEREST

THE BATMAN ADVENTURES:
MAD LOVE
DINI/TIMM

BATMAN:
THE DARK KNIGHT RETURNS
MILLER/JANSON/VARLEY

BATMAN: FACES
WAGNER

BATMAN:
THE KILLING JOKE
MOORE/BOLLAND/HIGGINS

BATMAN: YEAR ONE
MILLER/MAZZUCCHELLI/LEWIS

CAMELOT 3000
BARR/BOLLAND/VARIOUS

THE GOLDEN AGE
ROBINSON/SMITH

KINGDOM COME
WAID/ROSS

RONIN
MILLER

WATCHMEN
MOORE/GIBBONS